D1315805

Acknowledgments

The Authors and Publishers would like to thank Flic Eden for the Family Tree drawings, page 14; John and Penny Hubley, for the photographs on pages 32 (bottom) and 42; and the Government of India, Tourist Office, London, for the photographs on pages 38 (left), 43, 54 (bottom) and page 65. All the other photographs in the book were taken by John Ogle, who also drew the maps.

Typeset by Tek-Art Ltd, London SE20
and printed in Great Britain by
R.J. Acford
Chichester, Sussex
for the publishers
Batsford Academic and Educational Ltd,
an imprint of B.T. Batsford Ltd,
4 Fitzhardinge Street
London W1H 0AH

ISBN 0 7134 1227 5

Contents

Introduction

India is a vast country, a subcontinent of 700 million people which is made up of unimaginable extremes. It has some of the highest mountains in the world, extensive plains, deserts, jungles, tropical islands and, it seems, almost everything else between. Its people, too, come from very diverse cultures and can be far more different from each other than, for example, a Norwegian and an Italian. Hundreds of different dialects and fifteen distinct major languages are spoken. Many of them have their own scripts and so are as different from each other as English is from Greek.

Ancient India

The earliest known civilization in India* was in the Indus valley between 3000 and 1500 B.C. Many archaeological remains from this time have been found, including the great cities of Mohenjo Daro and Harappa. About 1500 B.C. the Indus was invaded by the Aryans, a warlike people from the north west. Over the next thousand years the *Vedas*, the most important Hindu religious texts, and the great epic poems, *Ramayana* and *Mahabharata* were compiled and with them came the formal development of Hinduism.

EXAMPLES OF SOME INDIAN SCRIPTS

English: What is your name ?

Hindi: आप का नाम क्या है ?

Urdu: تمہارا نام کیا ہے ؟

Gujarati: તમારૂ નામ શું છે ?

Malayalam: നിന്റെ പേര് എന്താണ്

---

* Before Independence (1947) "India" refers to the whole subcontinent, that is, including the areas now known as Pakistan and Bangladesh.

RACIAL TYPES

Most Indians belong to the Caucasian race although the other three ethnic stocks of the world are to be found, mainly in the tribal and Harijan population.

CAUCASIAN, *Nordic:* descendants of the Aryan invaders. Typically they are tall, light-skinned, high caste and live on the Indo-Gangetic plain.
Mediterranean: probably descendants of the people conquered by the Aryans. They are shorter, darker people, known as Dravidians, who live in South India, such as the Tamils.

MONGOLOID: pale, yellowish-skinned people with slanting eyes, living in the mountains and foothills east of Kashmir, such as Ladakhis and Assamese.

AUSTRALOID: small people who live in remote areas of central and south India, such as the Santals and Mundas.

NEGROID: small black people, mainly hunters and gatherers such as the Andaman Islanders and Kadars of Kerala.

Also during this time caste, which was originally a framework to cater for all the needs of a society, became a complex and rigid system. The Aryans eventually spread all over India taking with them the basic structure of Hindu society.

In the sixth century B.C. the Buddha was born and gave his teachings to the world.

5

Buddhism flourished in India for several hundred years and continues to do so in other parts of Asia.

Since the fourth century B.C. Northern India has been a succession of empires, the boundaries of which have changed many times. Until 1206 these had Hindu rulers except for one very famous emperor, Ashoka, who became a Buddhist. For the following 500 years the empire was ruled by Muslims. The Deccan, South India and some areas in the north were divided into many states independently ruled by princes.

During this time India was far from isolated, having connections both with the West, trading spices for precious metals with the Greek and Roman empires, and more importantly with the East, where India, with its Hindu and Buddhist traditions, has had an important part to play in the development of the civilizations of South East Asia, China and Japan.

Harijans in Madras. These women have picked through rubbish to find a few things that they can clean up and sell. The woman on the right has undone her "purse" — part of her sari knotted up to keep money — and is giving change of 5 paisa, a small square coin.

The Arrival of Islam

Islam came to India via its North-West frontier. Between 1000 and 1030 A.D. there were frequent invasions from the Islamic state of Afghanistan. Only the Punjab was taken, but the empire as a whole was considerably weakened. The next expansionist leader in Afghanistan was Mohammed of Ghor who, between 1190 and 1200, annexed the entire Indo-Gangetic plain. Since then, Islam has been important in all areas of Indian life. In 1206, close ties with Afghanistan were broken and a succession of dynasties known as the Delhi Sultanate ruled over Northern India until 1526.

The Moghuls

The Moghuls, descendants of the Mongol conquerors such as Genghis Khan, invaded the Punjab in 1526 and defeated the Sultan of Delhi. It took them thirty years to consolidate their claim to India and in 1556 Akbar, possibly the greatest ruler of India at any time, came to power. He attempted to build a secular state, encouraging the development of Hindu culture as well as Muslim, and so began a period in which all the arts flourished in India. One of Akbar's most important innovations was to allow Hindus to hold positions of authority which had been denied them since the Muslims came to power. His policies were continued until the reign of Aurangzeb (1658-1707), who increased the size of the empire but returned to the old repressive methods of earlier emperors. In reaction, many nationalist Hindu movements emerged in different parts of the country, the most important being the Marathas in the Western Ghats.

Europeans in India

The first Europeans to arrive in India were the Portuguese. Vasco da Gama landed in Calicut, Kerala, in 1498 and trading routes were established, taking spices to Europe. In 1510 Goa was captured. The political power of the Portuguese remained limited, however, to very small areas on the West Coast (Goa, Daman and Diu). In the seventeenth century they were followed to India by the Dutch and then by the British and French, who were also eager to establish their own trading centres and so break the Portuguese monopoly.

HISTORICAL PERIODS

Century	Event
6 B.C.	Life of Buddha and Mahavira, the founder of Jainism.
4 B.C.	Alexander the Great invades India.
4-2 B.C.	Mauryan dynasty rules the first North Indian empire. 273-232 B.C. Reign of Ashoka.
1-3 A.D.	Kushan dynasty rules North India.
4-5 A.D.	Gupta dynasty rules North India.
5-6 A.D.	Hun invasions.
5-9 A.D.	Pallava dynasty rules South India.
6-8 A.D.	Chalukya dynasty rules Deccan.
7-11 A.D.	Pala dynasty rules Bengal.
9-12 A.D.	Rajput kingdoms in Rajasthan.
9-13 A.D.	Chola dynasty rules South India.
11-16 A.D.	Delhi Sultanate rules North India. 1469-1538 Guru Nanak, founder of Sikhism.
14-16 A.D.	Vijayanagar dynasty rules part of Deccan.
14-17 A.D.	Bahmani (Muslim) dynasty rules part of Deccan.
16-17 A.D.	Moghuls rule North India. 1556-1605 Reign of Akbar. 1627-1658 Reign of Shah Jehan. 1658-1707 Reign of Aurangzeb.

The East India Company set up factories, first at Surat in 1612, then later at Bombay, Madras and Calcutta, where it became involved in Indian politics. By the eighteenth century, the Moghuls had lost much of their hold over India and nationalist movements in different parts of the country were making determined bids for independence. This political instability allowed the British and French to extend their claims. For over a hundred years there were wars all over India. By 1849 the British controlled almost the whole subcontinent, directly or through the allegiance of Indian rulers.

There was much resentment towards the British and in 1857 this exploded, with the mutiny of Indian army regiments at Meerut. Discontent spread rapidly and almost all of Northern India was up in arms. The mutiny was put down harshly and control moved from the East India Company to the British Government.

The years from 1858 to Independence in 1947 were very important for the unification of India and, although a large part of the country remained under the rule of Indian princes, most of them were forced to participate in the changes that were being systematically carried out by the British. An effective legislative code and administration were created, and road, rail, postal and telegraphic systems linked the country. Formal education became increasingly widespread, English being used as the unifying language.

In 1885, National Congress, the first Indian political party, was formed. Originally, it wanted Indian nationals to participate in the government, but this was not granted and Congress then became more extreme, pressing for Independence. In 1919 there was a terrible massacre at Jallianwalla Bagh, Amritsar, in which a huge, unarmed crowd holding a peaceful but illegal meeting was fired on by the British army. Nearly 400 people were killed and over 1000 more, seriously injured. This incident greatly increased resentment against the British and Mahatma Gandhi joined the national struggle.

He set up a programme of non-cooperation with the government and it was gradually accepted that Home Rule for India would have to become a reality.

The issue was then complicated by disagreements in the National Congress. One problem was how to include the large areas still ruled by princes, so that the new country could be a cohesive unit, for some of the princes did not want to give up their territories. Another problem was that, led by Mohammed Ali Jinnah, the Muslims, who formed a majority in several states of Northern India, wanted to form a separate country. Eventually, most of the princely states acceded to India and on 15 August 1947 the subcontinent was divided into two independent states — India and Pakistan. Pakistan was in two separate parts, to the west and east of Northern India. East Pakistan became a country in its own right in 1971 and was renamed Bangladesh. This division was not achieved without much bloodshed during the great migrations as millions of Hindus, Sikhs and Muslims crossed the new borders.

Since Independence

The Republic of India, with its new constitution, was declared on 26 January 1950. The constitution was formulated after many studies had been made of democracies in different parts of the world and of how they could be applied to India's situation. The Indian constitution states that the economic system should operate for everyone's benefit and that the interests of weaker sections of society, the scheduled castes and tribals, should be furthered. India is a secular state and discrimination on grounds of religion, caste or sex is forbidden.

India is governed on a federal system and now has 22 states and 9 union territories. The Central Parliament, known as the Lok Sabha, has 500 members who are elected by the whole country for a five-year term. There are also State elections every five

At election time, signs such as this are painted all over the place. The fish is the symbol of the political party to which Abdul belongs. Each party has a symbol, which appears on the ballot paper, making it possible for illiterate people to know for whom they are voting.

years to choose the members of the State Legislatures. The Council of States, or Rajya Sabha, has 250 members and operates in a similar way to the British House of Lords, except that its members are not hereditary but elected by the State Legislatures and serve for six years. The Rajya Sabha is never dissolved, one third of its members being replaced every two years. The Head of State is the President, who is elected by both Houses of Parliament (Lok Sabha and Rajya Sabha) and the State Legislatures. Real power, though, is held by the Prime Minister, the leader of the Party holding a majority in Parliament.

In 1952, the Congress Party led by Jawaharlal Nehru was voted in and the government of Independent India began with a policy of very high ideals in its struggle against poverty. Although much has been achieved since Independence, there is still an enormous difference between rich and poor, and many customs, officially banned, persist in practice. The popularity of the Congress Party has continued and it has been constantly re-elected, except for a period between 1977 and 1980. In 1975 Mrs Gandhi, its leader, was accused of corruption. Leaders of the opposition parties were arrested, however, and the country was declared to be in a state of emergency. New laws were introduced that resulted in censorship of the press and mass arrests. Many people doubted that India would remain a democracy, but in March 1977 Mrs Gandhi ended the emergency and called an election. The Congress Party lost and was succeeded by the Janata Party Coalition led by Morarji Desai. The new government and its successor were not able to rule successfully, and in 1980 the people of India again voted for the strong leadership of Mrs Gandhi.

9

January

Calendars

There are many different ways of measuring time and, in India, the Gregorian calendar is followed only for official purposes. So, for most people, the first of January has no particular significance and is not celebrated. A national calendar was adopted in 1957 in addition to the Gregorian, and is used by the national newspapers and All India Radio and for government communications with the public. Its New Year falls on 22 March. Most people, though, follow their traditional calendars, which vary in different parts of the country. New Year is therefore celebrated at different times according to which part of India you are in. Hindu calendars are calculated according to both lunar and solar changes, so the dates of most festivals vary

each year, although they generally fall in the same season. According to Hindu calculations, we are now in the era of creation, year 1,972,949,083 (1982 A.D.).

Pongal

We shall start our year in India in the south, the state of Tamil Nadu. The rains are over

Well-dressed young Tamil women. Girls often wear Western-style dresses until they reach their early teens, when they start wearing a sari. The little girl has a garland of sweet-smelling flowers in her hair.

Tamil Nadu

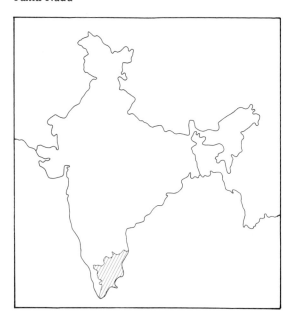

Decorated cow.

and it is the cool season, which means that it is pleasantly warm in most places and there are frosts only high in the hills. The countryside is a patchwork of green and gold. Low mud walls, which are used as pathways, divide the small fields and there are clumps of palm trees breaking up the flat landscape. The rice, to which almost all the fields are devoted, is at several different stages of growth. Some has already been harvested, while most of it has just been planted out from nursery beds, a tiring job done by the women, whose fingers rapidly secure the long, bright green seedlings deep in the mud.

About the middle of January, the Tamils hold a big thanksgiving festival which lasts three days and is known as Pongal. On the first day of the festival, bonfires are made in the villages and a special pudding is cooked using freshly harvested rice. Although rice is the most important part of every meal in South India, it is rarely eaten as a sweet, so this is a seasonal treat and much enjoyed by everyone. On the second day the sun, which has helped make the rice grow, is thanked. On the third day of Pongal, cows and bullocks are honoured. Their horns are painted bright colours and often tipped with brass ornaments. Garlands of flowers are hung round their necks and they are fed on a thick rice porridge made with sugar cane juice. In the afternoon, there is a procession and the cows are led round the village, accompanied by loud drumming and music. Everyone joins in and has fun, especially the children who are allowed to run around and do as they like.

Cows are often seen wandering about in the street by themselves or just resting, as these are.

The Importance of Cows

There are many Hindu gods and one of the most important is Brahma, Creator of the Universe. He is said to have created cows and Brahmins, the highest or priestly caste, at the same time: Brahmins, to conduct religious ceremonies, and cows, to provide materials necessary for the rituals, such as *ghee* (clarified butter), milk and curds. Cows are therefore regarded as the most sacred of all animals. They are never killed by Hindus and in all states of India, except West Bengal and Kerala, it is against the law for anyone to kill a cow.

Although they are sacred, cattle are regarded as useful working animals. Bullocks pull ploughs and carts; cows provide calves and milk which, as many Indians are completely vegetarian, is an important although small part of their diet. Cattle also provide dung which is used as manure and fuel, and the skins of dead animals are cured to provide leather. Although cows are regarded so highly, no special fodder crops are grown because of the shortage of land and they survive on straw, vegetable peelings and a little grass.

Family Life

Households are generally large in India. When a man marries, he brings his new wife to live in his parents' house so there are often several families living together. The

Cow dung is mixed with straw and pressed out into flat cakes which are left to dry in the sun to provide a good, slow-burning fuel.

head of the household is usually the oldest man and he takes care of the finances, receiving all income into a central pool and then sharing it out as he thinks best. His wife is also an important person within the family group because she is in charge of all the younger women and their activities, making sure that all the work is done. This communal way of living ensures that people are not lonely and that tasks are shared. Children have playmates and old people continue to help run the home as long as they are able and, if necessary, have plenty of people to look after them.

The extended family system generally worked well when sons naturally followed their father's occupation and stayed in their own villages. Increasingly, however, as more highly paid work is to be found in towns and cities, young people move away from their family homes and set up on their own. As ways of thinking change, young people are also less willing to accept rules laid down by the older generation and want more freedom than is possible at home. When they grow old, parents often move to the towns to live with their children.

Home

Because wealth is unequally distributed in India there are enormous differences in how and where people live. A very few live in great luxury, but, apart from this small elite,

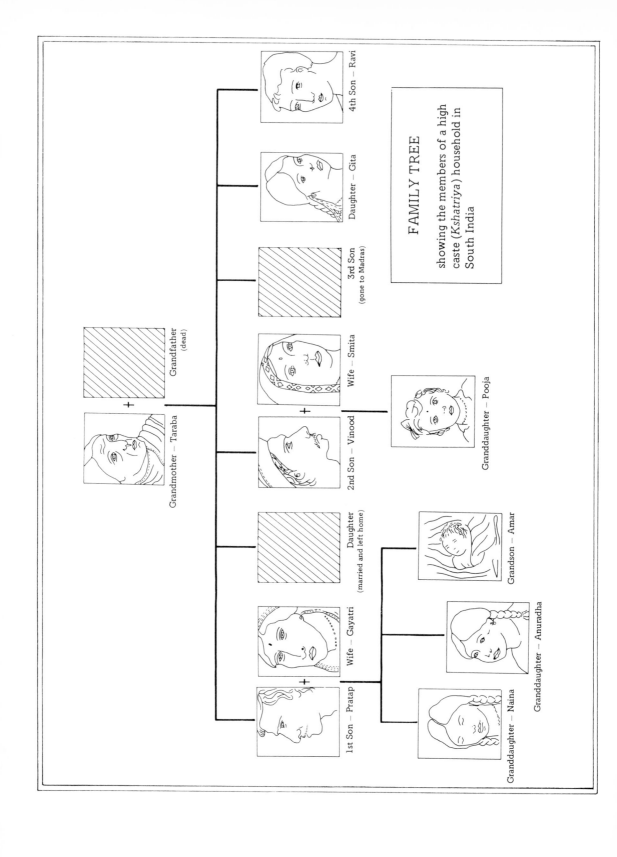

FAMILY TREE

showing the members of a high caste (*Kshatriya*) household in South India

Grandfather (dead) + Grandmother – Taraba

4th Son – Ravi

Daughter – Gita

3rd Son (gone to Madras)

Wife – Smita + 2nd Son – Vinood

Granddaughter – Pooja

Daughter (married and left home)

1st Son – Pratap + Wife – Gayatri

Grandson – Amar

Granddaughter – Anuradha

Granddaughter – Naina

Indian homes, even of the moderately affluent, are simple, with a minimum of furniture.

The floor is tiled, concrete or beaten earth. It is swept several times a day and kept very clean. You leave your shoes at the door and sit inside on a mat on the floor or there may be a *charpoy*, a wooden-framed bed strung with rope or cane, to lounge on. At one end of the room there is probably a small shrine with brightly coloured pictures of the family's favourite gods. Flowers and sticks of incense are placed in front of the pictures, as offerings.

The most usual way of greeting people is to place your hands together and say "Namaste" or "Namaskar". This woman wears her sari in a style common in North India, in which the free end is brought over the right shoulder from the back and then tucked in on the left side.

Sewage pipe being laid in an outlying district of Trivandrum, Kerala.

In all but the poorest homes there is a separate kitchen with a fireplace, a large waterpot, a metal box to keep grain safe from rats and insects, a few pots and pans, a mill for grinding grain and a mortar and pestle for spices. Visitors should never enter someone's kitchen unless specifically invited to do so, as orthodox Hindus follow very strict rules of hygiene that you may unknowingly break. Relatively wealthy people in towns have water piped to their houses, but very few people have hot water, as it is unnecessary and expensive. Women in the villages, and many in towns too, have to go to fetch their water in large pots carried on their heads from a communal tap, pump or well.

In the bathroom there is a large bucket of water and a dipper which you use to pour water over yourself. The floor is usually slightly sloping and the water disappears out of a hole in one corner. The toilet does not have a seat but is two foot rests either side of the bowl over which you squat. People often have to share these facilities with many others or do not have access to them at all.

Republic Day

26 January is Republic Day, which commemorates India's becoming a Federal Republic with a democratic constitution in 1950. It is celebrated in all the state capitals, but is most spectacular in New Delhi. It is much cooler here than it was in Tamil Nadu,

16

but cold only at night. There is a huge military display with soldiers on foot and horseback, on camels and elephants, and in tanks and aeroplanes. The route taken by the procession is packed with people, squeezing in wherever they can find a tiny space for themselves. Great ingenuity is shown by those who are keen to have a good view. The military parade is followed by all kinds of others, such as the civil services which include the police force, fire brigades and several women's organizations. There are also extravagantly decorated floats, musicians and folk dancers. The procession ends with the President of India taking the salute, and aeroplanes overhead set off orange, white and green flares, the colours of the Indian flag.

February

Hinduism and God

Unlike most other religions, Hinduism has neither founder nor definite creed. It is very comprehensive, all kinds of belief and behaviour being accepted as possible ways of reaching God. Because of this, Hindus are generally tolerant of other religions. The main principles of Hinduism are to seek the Truth and not to injure any living being. Beyond that, everyone is free to experience God in his own way. In practice, some generalizations can be made, but there are so many different beliefs that these can only be said to be true of some Hindus in some places.

God is considered to be everywhere, without form and neither male nor female, an unlimited energy which encompasses not only this world but many others too. In Sanskrit, God is known as Brahman and is invoked by using the word *Om.*

Gods and Goddesses

Besides this understanding of one universal God, Hindus also have a rich and intricate

The sacred OM is seen and heard wherever you go in India. It is regarded as the original sound of the universe and symbolizes the completeness of God.

mythology. There are hundreds of gods and goddesses who are regarded as manifestations of God, which are sent to help people find the universal God. Most Hindus, therefore, have a personal god or goddess such as Shiva, Krishna or Lakshmi to whom they pray regularly.

There are three principal gods to whom most of the others are connected in some way. They are Brahma, known as the

Creator, Vishnu, the Preserver and Shiva, the Destroyer. Brahma is not worshipped very much and there is only one temple dedicated to him in the whole of India. He has a wife, Saraswati, who is the goddess of learning and the arts. There are many followers of Vishnu and his wife Lakshmi, the goddess of prosperity, who is the patron of the Vaishya (merchant) caste. Vishnu has ten incarnations and two of them, Rama and Krishna, are widely worshipped in their own right. Shiva also has many followers and is considered the most powerful of all the gods. He is the terrible god of destruction who overcomes all ignorance and illusion, the main causes of evil in the world. Shiva and his wife, Parvati, are also known by many other names according to different roles that they play; for example, Nataraj is Shiva as the cosmic dancer. Durga is the destructive side of Parvati. They have a son, Ganesh, who is the god of prudence and prosperity and is easily recognizable because he has an elephant's head.

Karma and Rebirth

Karma applies throughout life and means that a person's past deeds have brought him to his present position in life; and what he does now will determine the course of his life in future. Death is regarded as a stage on the way to reincarnation in another body. The new body will be born in a situation corresponding to the karma of the past life. The soul is working towards perfection and only when Enlightenment comes will it cease to be reincarnated. In India, as this life is regarded only as a transitory phase, great importance is attached to the spirit.

Temples

You cannot go very far in India without coming across a temple or shrine. Wayside shrines are often just a stone daubed with red powder and strewn with flowers in the shade of a peepul tree (Ficus religiosa).

Temples can be small and simple, with an image of just one god, or a huge complex which has hundreds of different shrines around the inner sanctum, where the image of the god or goddess to whom the temple is dedicated is kept. These great temples are looked after by thousands of priests and also house many animals, such as elephants and sometimes camels, which take part in the processions. They may also have their own stalls inside, selling offerings, incense, sandalwood paste and religious pictures.

Before entering a temple, you slip off your sandals and there is usually a man outside who looks after them. Inside the temple there is always somewhere to wash, either a big waterpot, a row of taps or there may be a huge pool known as a tank, with steps going down into it. You always wash to purify yourself, both physically and symbolically, before praying. Hindus generally prefer to bathe in flowing water, so, if there is a river nearby, they go there to wash before coming to the temple.

Puja or worship is an individual matter and there are no services which have to be attended. Although there is no obligation and many people stay at home to say their prayers, sunrise is a busy time at the temple as it is considered the best time of day to pray. Musicians play and huge shells are blown like trumpets to awaken the gods and after visiting various shrines on the way to the main god, you take your offerings of flowers,

---

A PRAYER

This prayer concludes all ceremonies: Peace be in the higher worlds: peace be in the firmament; peace be on earth. May the waters flow peacefully; may the herbs and shrubs grow peacefully; may all the divine powers bring us peace. Brahman, the Supreme, is peace. May all be in peace, in peace and only peace; and may that peace come to me. OM. Peace, Peace, Peace.

incense, ghee, fruit or money and with your right hand give them to the priest who then performs complicated rituals. After praying, the priest sometimes gives out *prasad*, food, which is usually something sweet, that has been blessed.

Shivratri

At new moon in February, there is the important festival of Shivratri. It is one of the few festivals that is purely religious, as most include a lot of fun and entertainment besides prayer. All over India, followers of Shiva go to his temples and spend the night chanting and singing. The most well-known

Varanasi is a city of many temples. The flights of steps going down into the river are known as ghats and it is possible to walk the whole length of Varanasi, along the bank of the Ganga, crossing from one ghat to another. There is a special ghat reserved for cremations and vultures are an inevitable part of the scene.

Shiva temples are in Varanasi in Uttar Pradesh, Khajuraho in Madhya Pradesh, and Chidambaram in Tamil Nadu.

Varanasi

Varanasi or Benares is India's holiest city and centre of Shiva worship. It is built on

19

the banks of the Ganga (Ganges), India's most sacred river whose waters are said to have the power of washing away sins. Every devout Hindu hopes to visit Varanasi at least once in his lifetime and if possible be there when he dies. Every year, millions of pilgrims go to Varanasi and many of the older ones stay there, awaiting death.

It is a higgledy-piggledy city of many winding alleys, tiny shops and stalls. Cycle rickshaws, pedestrians, cows, bulls and water buffaloes all try to make their way along the narrow cobbled streets. Suddenly the view opens out onto the clear, wide river with

---

MUNDAN

Mundan or head shaving ceremony happens when a child is about one year old and symbolizes the removal of any bad karma that might have been brought from a past life. It is sometimes done later in life too, as a special sacrifice, especially when on pilgrimage.

Different kinds of gourds, marrow-like vegetables, for sale in Varanasi.

fields on the other side; a great contrast to all the noise and activity of the city. For about two miles along the river bank are the *ghats*, steep steps going down to the water, and before dawn people are already taking their purifying bath. Many priests are seated near the water's edge under huge straw sunshades waiting to aid the pilgrims with their prayers. Barbers are also an important part of the scene, shaving faces and often heads too, and there are always beggars hoping that a few coins will come their way.

Funerals are frequent events in Varanasi and always take place soon after death. The body is wrapped in a white cloth, placed on a stretcher and covered with garlands of flowers. It is then carried by the mourners who chant all the way down to the burning *ghat*. A large pyre is built and the body cremated. Twelve days after the funeral, the family has a special meal in memory of the person who died. In India, white is the colour of mourning and if a woman is widowed, she will wear a white sari, no jewellery or make-up and is not supposed to remarry.

Although the Ganga is used to dispose of the dead, for bathing, washing clothes and

also receives untreated sewage at several places, its water is extraordinarily clear and is regarded as completely pure. The river's ability to purify itself is confirmed by modern science and the water is remarkably free from harmful bacteria.

Dead man covered in garlands of flowers, just before his funeral. Oil lamps, candles and agar bathi (sticks of incense) are kept burning around the body.

March

Holi

March sees the end of the cool season and, to welcome spring, there is a very colourful festival throughout Northern India called Holi, which is celebrated on the day after the full moon. It is an occasion to renew old friendships, forget disputes and make new friends. During the week leading up to Holi, you have to be careful when out on the street, as practical jokers are everywhere and, however watchful you are, sooner or later you will be drenched by a water bomb thrown by some boys hidden on a roof or behind a wall.

On the night of the full moon, large bonfires are lit and everyone congregates to talk and make jokes. Holi itself is celebrated wearing old clothes. In the morning you go out to find your friends, taking with you several small packets of brightly coloured powder. Electric blue and shocking pink are particular favourites. Meeting someone, you ask if they are playing Holi, then hug and paint each other's forehead and cheeks with the powders. There are children everywhere, armed with large syringes full of coloured water, squirting passers-by.

By midday, everyone, the streets, walls and animals are covered with vivid streaks of colour. The hilarity stops abruptly at one o'clock, as everyone goes home to wash and change. The afternoon is spent more quietly enjoying a rest and a meal with friends.

Hola

At Anandpur Sahib, in the Punjab, the following day is known as Hola Mohalla and is a Sikh celebration. In their martial tradition, Sikhs fight mock battles using traditional weapons and afterwards there is a festival of folk music and dancing.

Farming in the Punjab

Before Independence and the creation of Pakistan, the Punjab was a very large, wealthy state, known as the land of five rivers and the granary of India. Partition badly disrupted life, as half the Punjab now belonged to Pakistan, and Muslims in the eastern part of the state crossed the new border, while Hindus and Sikhs in the west travelled in the opposite direction. Millions of displaced people had to find new homes and livelihoods. Also, the irrigation systems, which diverted water from the great rivers to the fields and played such an important part in obtaining good harvests, had to be completely reorganized to accommodate the needs of

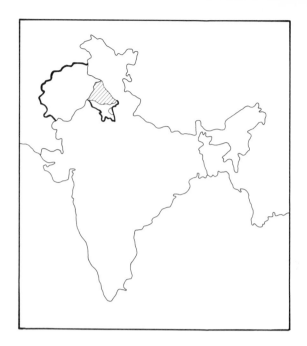

▨ Punjab Today

— Punjab Before Independence

both India and Pakistan. In spite of these difficulties, the new Punjab and Harayana (which was also part of the Punjab until 1966) are again one of India's richest agricultural areas.

The fertile land is intensively farmed and, as in the rest of India, the emphasis is on growing cereals. Here it is mainly wheat. Other important crops are pulses (beans and lentils), sesame and mustard seeds which are crushed for oil, and sugar cane. There are also many wild date palms which are tapped at the top of the trunk for the sweet juice which is made into *jaggery*, another kind of sugar. Farms are generally small, but agricultural co-operatives have been successfully formed in the Punjab, and scattered smallholdings consolidated into more economic units.

The day starts very early for most people. About 5.00 a.m., well before dawn, people are stirring, noisily clearing their throats, cleaning their teeth with a twig from the

22

Cutting sugar cane into manageable lengths. There are stalls in most towns where sugar cane is crushed in a small machine like a mangle, to extract the juice. It is a very refreshing drink, especially when a little lime juice or crushed ginger is added, to bring out its flavour.

23

Teashops are found all over India and are popular meeting places. The urn contains a long cylinder in which pieces of charcoal burn, to heat the water. Milk and sugar are added to the water while the tea is being made, rather than afterwards. Here the tea is being poured quickly from one beaker to the other so that some froth is formed on top. It will then be served in a glass. The man is wearing a lungi, an ankle-length piece of coloured cloth which is wrapped around the body like a long skirt. Often, the lungi is then folded up and tucked in so that it only reaches the knees, as here. This is the traditional dress for men in South India.

neem tree, washing and saying prayers. After a cup of sweet milky tea, the men go out to the fields. At the moment, the wheat is almost ready for harvesting. It is nearly all cut and bundled by hand, then it is laid out in a circle in a flat, open place and a pair of bullocks trample over it, dragging a heavy wooden rake behind them. Slowly, the wheat is broken up and when it is all in small pieces, the women put it on slatted trays which they wave above their heads so that the grains of wheat fall straight down and the chaff flies away to the sides.

Women's Work

Village women always work very hard. They are first up in the morning and are busy lighting a fire to make tea or sweeping the house by the time the children and men stir. Water and firewood have to be collected and carried home, clothes have to be washed and food cooked. Preparing the food always takes a long time, as the wheat and lentils have to be carefully picked over to remove small stones, before they can be used, and many things are done at home using simple handpowered tools — for example, churning butter, grinding spices and sometimes flour. In the middle of the morning, the women go to the fields, taking some food for their husbands, and then often stay there to work until the afternoon when they go home to prepare the evening meal.

Food

Punjabi food relies heavily on different kinds of flatbread, which are accompanied by a variety of spiced vegetables, a thick soup of split peas or lentils called *dhal*, or curried

◁ A special pot or bucket is used to draw water from the well and then the water is transferred to the larger pot. There are often some large stones or a concreted area near the well, where women wash the clothes, beating them hard to loosen the dirt.

24

Woman making chapattis. *She quickly establishes a rhythm of rolling out a ball of dough while the other* chapatti *is cooking. It only takes about a minute to cook. After the* chapatti *has puffed up, she throws it onto the pile keeping warm in front of the fire. Most work in the kitchen is done either sitting down or squatting, using equipment on the floor, which is kept very clean.*

Man selling curd (yoghurt). The curd in North India is particularly rich. The pot behind is used for making lassi, *a delicious, cooling drink made from curd and water with a little sugar or salt added. The wooden stick going through the lid is the handle of a whisk and is rubbed quickly between the hands to make the whisk rotate and beat the* lassi *until it is smooth. All kinds of brilliantly coloured soft drinks are popular, but relatively expensive in India.*

FLATBREADS

1. *CHAPATTIS*: thin circles of wholemeal dough which are rolled out and usually cooked on an iron plate over the fire. When almost cooked, they are held near the embers of the fire, so that they puff up like a ball for a moment and form two separate layers.
2. *NAN*: large oval-shaped loaves which are sometimes leavened with yeast. They are baked on the walls of a clay oven known as a *tandoor.*
3. *PARATHAS*: similar to *chapattis,* but brushed with ghee, so that they are much richer. *Parathas* are sometimes stuffed with vegetables or meat and are usually triangular in shape.
4. *ROTIS*: similar to *parathas,* but made with white flour and slightly leavened.
5. *PURIS*: small, deep-fried *chapattis.*

meat which is often mutton, and several kinds of chutney and pickle.

Punjabis are generally tall and well-built and regard themselves as the strongest people in India, attributing their strength partly to their good diet of wheat and meat.

Before eating, you always wash your hands carefully, as it is polite to eat with the fingers of the right hand. Indians like to feel the texture of their food and think that metal forks or spoons can spoil its flavour. Pieces of *chapatti* are torn off and used to scoop up the different curries. They all have very distinctive tastes which are predominantly sweet, bitter, salty, sour, pungent or astringent. It is considered that a balance of these is necessary to keep healthy and food is usually eaten warm, as extremes of temperature are bad for the digestion. Desserts are eaten only on special occasions. After the meal, you wash your hands again and rinse out your mouth. In traditional homes men usually eat on their own and the women enjoy their meal later, without having to attend to everybody else's needs while trying to eat.

Parsees

Two important minority groups have their main festivals of the year this month.

Many Zoroastrians left Persia in the seventh century because they were being persecuted by the Muslim majority. They settled around Bombay and became known as the Parsees. They have many temples in Bombay, and in each a sacred fire burns, which is regarded as the manifestation of God. Their holy book, the Zend Avesta, teaches a path of action, overcoming evil by good thoughts, words and deeds. When a Parsee dies, his body is placed at the top of the Towers of Silence, where hordes of vultures dispose of it, as this is considered preferable to polluting the ground by burying the body or the air by cremating it. The Parsees have made important contributions to industrial success in India, including the great firm of Tata, which has very wide commercial interests including a steel works, and many different light industries such as engineering and toiletries. 21 March is Jamshed Navroz, Parsee New Year, which is celebrated by going to the temple and then, at home, feasting and having fun with friends.

Jains

At the end of March or the beginning of April is Mahavir Jayanti, the birthday of Mahavira, who lived in the sixth century B.C. at about the same time as the Buddha. Mahavira taught that salvation could be attained by leading an extremely ascetic life, strictly limiting all wants and desires. His other important instruction was that you should be completely harmless to all life. Jains, therefore, avoid fighting, fishing and farming, are strict vegetarians and do not eat root vegetables or anything red, the colour of blood. They often wear a white mask over their nose and mouth, to prevent accidentally breathing in and killing small insects. The Jains are a wealthy community, renowned for their resourcefulness and business acumen.

April

Spring in Kashmir

The arrival of spring is especially welcome in Kashmir, as winters are long and hard. In Srinagar, the spring festival starts at the end of March or beginning of April, when the almond blossom appears and wild flowers cover the valley. Everyone goes off to the orchards which surround Dal Lake, taking elaborate picnics with them. Prominent in all

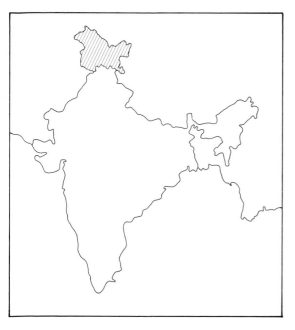

Jammu and Kashmir

Moghul emperors who stayed there for the hot season, as they did not like the heat and dust of the plains. They laid out the most beautiful formal gardens, which included many channels for running water and fountains. Kashmir has continued to be a select holiday resort, but, because of its distance from the main centres on the plains, never became like the British hill stations further east.

During British rule of India, Jammu and Kashmir were governed as a semi-autonomous state by the Maharaja. Europeans were not allowed to own land in the state, which led to the British keeping houseboats on Dal Lake. The houseboats are still there and, during the busy tourist season from April to October, they are used as holiday homes for the wealthy. Kashmiri handicrafts are famous throughout India, particularly the

the paraphernalia necessary for a good picnic are the large, ornate pots in which the tea, sweet and spiced or sometimes salty, is brewed. Kashmiris use a special kind of tea which has a very distinctive flavour.

Kashmir has always been renowned for its beauty and was very popular with the

Cobbler. The second-hand shoes on the left of the picture are for sale. Hardly anything is wasted in India and belongings are always mended and re-mended rather than thrown away. Most things are recycled — for example, old tyres are often used to sole shoes, large tins are hammered flat and used for roofing, and old exercise books are torn up to make paper bags.

There are few beasts of burden in the mountains and men often carry enormous loads. Goods are generally carried in cone-shaped baskets which, like this boiler, are supported by a strap round the forehead.

fine, exquisitely embroidered shawls, cream-coloured rugs embroidered with flowers, and papier mâché bowls decorated with intricate designs in gold leaf.

Most people in Kashmir are Muslim, but the Maharaja and leading minority were Hindu, which caused problems when India became independent and Pakistan was created. The Maharaja eventually decided to join India, but most people wished the state to become part of Pakistan. Kashmir has continued to be a cause of dispute between the two countries and there have been three wars, two of them over Kashmir.

Hill Stations

The hill stations, such as Simla, Dalhousie, Mussoorie and Naini Tal in the foothills of the Himalayas and Ootacamund and Kodaikanal in South India, were developed

The milkman. Pahari men often wear caps — this ▷ style comes from near the Kulu valley in Himachal Pradesh. Men also wear thick waistcoats or brown tweed jackets.

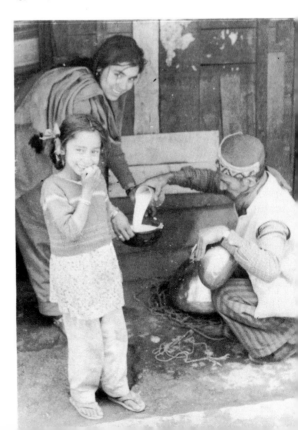

British church in Kodaikanal, Tamil Nadu.

by the British as places of respite from the heat of the plains, which becomes intense during April and May. Originally, they were ordinary villages, but have had English towns added on, with churches, schools, playing fields and large houses with spacious gardens, growing all kinds of English flowers. The hill stations continue to be a haven for wealthy Indians, and a relaxed, holiday atmosphere prevails, which contrasts sharply with the hardworking lives led by the *paharis* (hill-people) and the other inhabitants of the mountains, the religious hermits, who go there for peace and solitude.

Paharis are generally very sturdy, energetic people, with light skins and often grey eyes. The hills are covered with huge red-flowered rhododendrons and, at this time of year, there are several *melas* or fairs. The sound of drums and horns echoes through the hills and the local gods are taken from their temples to watch the festivities, which include a lot of music and folk dancing.

The Himalayas

Across the entire land frontier of northern India, for a distance of 1600 miles, runs the highest range of mountains in the world, the Himalayas. Their name means "the abode of snows", as the high valleys and mountain peaks are white all year round. There are three ranges running parallel to each other. The furthest south and lowest are the Siwalik Hills. Separating the Siwaliks from the middle range, the Lesser Himalaya, are long valleys called *duns*, which are generally intensively farmed. The highest range is the Greater Himalaya, which has many peaks over 6000 metres, and on its northern side falls to the Tibetan Plateau.

The mountains form an important barrier which shuts off India from the rest of Asia

29

and modifies its climate and vegetation. The Himalayas also have a strong influence on the people of the subcontinent, as they are considered to be the home of the gods, and the snows represent eternity and the Hindu ideal of serene detachment from worldly matters.

This month many people start on pilgrimages to the shrines high in the mountains. The places most frequently visited during April and May are Gangotri, believed to be the source of the river Ganga; Badrinath, which is the god Vishnu's sanctuary; and Kedarnath, dedicated to Shiva.

Baisakhi

13 April is Baisakhi, solar new year according to the Hindu calendar. Although most of India celebrates new year at different times, Baisakhi is still celebrated throughout Northern India and Tamil Nadu, because the river Ganga is believed to have descended to earth on this day. In the Punjab, Baisakhi is especially important, since there, it is regarded as New Year's Day and the Sikhs remember it as the day on which, in 1699, their last guru, Gobind Singh, formed the Khalsa, the martial brotherhood to which most Sikhs belong. Baisakhi is also a harvest festival celebrated with a lot of music and dancing. Public address systems are set up in the towns and villages, and music is played over loudspeakers. The traditional dance at Baisakhi is the Bhangra, which is danced by men and celebrates an abundant harvest.

It is extremely hot this month in most of India, and everything is dry and dusty. People put their beds on the roof or outside, as it is much pleasanter to sleep under the stars than in the stifling house. Farmers are ploughing their fields in readiness for the rain, when they can start planting. One compensation in the heat and dust is the mangos, which are at the height of their season now. They are a fragrant, sweet, juicy fruit with firm flesh that varies from yellow to deep apricot in colour. The skin is green, sometimes tinged with orange or red, and mango trees are very large and beautiful, offering welcome shade from the sun.

Meenakshi Kalyanam

At the beginning of May there is a big festival at the great Meenakshi temple in Madurai, Tamil Nadu. It lasts ten days and celebrates the marriage of the goddess Meenakshi, another name of Parvati, to the great god Shiva. The wedding is enacted in the temple and then the images of Meenakshi and Shiva are taken out on a large colourful chariot, which is accompanied by an enormous procession, including all the temple elephants which are heavily decorated, priests, musicians and thousands of people chanting sacred songs. The procession makes its way around the streets of Madurai and eventually returns to the temple, where the images are reinstalled.

Marriage

In India, a marriage is more like an alliance

of families than of individuals and is almost always arranged by the parents. It is generally believed that the parents are much better able to make a good match for their child, as they know him or her very well and can see clearly, without the distortion of youthful infatuation, who would be a suitable partner. Prospective partners are chosen from the same caste and background, as a rule, and horoscopes are carefully checked by an astrologer, to make sure that the young couple are compatible. Weddings are invariably noisy, joyous occasions which last for several days, and the families go to an immense amount of trouble and expense to

◁ *Two of the gopurams (towers) of the Meenakshi temple, Madurai. They are covered with ornate, brightly coloured sculptures of gods and goddesses from top to bottom. In the foreground, steps going down into the tank can be seen. This style of temple architecture is seen only in South India.*

MARRIAGE ADVERTS— MALE AND FEMALE
THE HINDUSTAN TIMES WEEKLY
MATRIMONIALS

WANTED Officer or well settled business-man for 24 yrs., 155 cms., M.A., whea-tish complexioned, smart and homely, Brahmin girl. Early decent marriage. Apply Box . . .

MATCH for homely, sophisticated Punjabi issueless, divorcee Teachress having white patches (not on face), earning 1000 asset for deserving family. No bars. Particulars with photo to . . .

FOR BEAUTIFUL, convent educated, cul-tured, M.A., virgin, 44/162, of Punjabi Khatri, high/respectable family, well set-tled/educated, 44-50, from any caste/pro-vince/Europeans can be considered, Box . . .

MATCH preferably MBA, Engineer, Doctor for Arora MBBS girl, doing P.G. Diploma, 25 years, 155 cms. Box . . .

BEAUTIFUL, educated tall girl for Kayasth bachelor, businessman, 35, 181 cms., month-ly income above Rs 5000/-, possess good urban property, maintain a Car. Early marriage. Caste no bar. Box . . .

MATCH for vegetarian, Punjabi Brahmin Graduate Govt. service, 27/162/900/-, Only son. Box . . .

WANTED beautiful, homely girl, willing to settle Philippines for 22/170, handsome Punjabi boy, having own business, Manila citizen, owning house, South Delhi. Early marriage. Box . . .

JAT, VERY beautiful, educated bride for handsome, healthy Jat boy, 28/167, Govt. job, 1300, own house, South Delhi. Box . . .

Applying henna, using a stencil. Usually, the designs are drawn freehand with a stick. Henna leaves are ground to a pulp, which is left on the hands for several hours before washing it off. Reddish-brown patterns remain and the design lasts for about a month.

The man in the centre of the photograph is counting out money, which is being handed over as part of the dowry at a Hindu wedding. The men are sitting on charpoys.

ensure a good start to their children's life together.

The bride is prepared for her wedding by her mother and other female members of the family. She is massaged with scented oils to make her hair and skin smooth and silky, and a paste of turmeric, and sometimes other herbs, is applied to her face, to improve and lighten her complexion, as fair skin is considered beautiful. Her eyes are darkened with kajal, a black paste or powder which is thought to be good for the eyes, besides being decorative, and designs are painted with henna on her hands and feet. She is then carefully dressed in a red sari and wears as much jewellery as possible. Gold is worn only on the upper part of the body and silver on the feet and ankles.

Both the bride and groom wear large garlands of flowers and there are many rituals to bind the young couple together. The groom puts a spot of red powder on his bride's forehead and also some in the parting of her hair. He than puts a gold necklace on her which is also a sign that she is now a married woman.

It is still usual for a girl to bring a dowry with her when she marries, although in 1961 a law was passed to stop the custom. The dowry is an insurance for the girl to be well cared for in her new home, usually her husband's parents' house. Now that women often work outside the home and have their own income, it is not so important.

Buddha Purnima

The eve of the full moon in May marks the birth, enlightenment and death of the Buddha and there are special celebrations at Buddh Gaya and Sarnath, the main centres of Buddhist pilgrimage in India.

Ladakh

Apart from Sikkim, which was annexed in 1975, Ladakh is the only region of India whose population is predominantly Buddhist. The Ladakhis follow Tibetan Buddhism and regard the Dalai Lama as their spiritual leader. Politically, Ladakh is part of Jammu and Kashmir State, but is sometimes known as little Tibet, as its cultural ties are with Tibet, rather than India. The region is mostly mountainous desert, having extreme temperatures and only three or four inches of rain a year. Life can be supported on a minute proportion of the land, mainly along the river valleys. Ladakh became important to India after the Chinese assumed control of Tibet in 1950 and there were serious disputes over boundaries, both here and in Arunachal Pradesh in the north east. An airport was built in Leh, Ladakh's largest town, so that troops and provisions could be transported there, as the road link with Srinagar can only be used between May and November.

Tibetans in India

When the Chinese came to Tibet, a unique way of life which had continued for centuries, completely isolated from the rest of the world, was suddenly forced to change. In 1959 the Dalai Lama, spiritual and temporal leader of Tibet, escaped to India. He has been followed by about 80,000 people and still some continue to cross the high passes into India, in spite of Chinese attempts to close the border.

The Dalai Lama now lives near Dharamsala, Himachal Pradesh, in a village higher up the mountain, called McCleod Ganj. The Tibetans have brought some of their culture with them: clothes, food, medicine, music, dancing and, most importantly, their religion, but, as refugees, they can no longer maintain their traditional way of life. Many Tibetans now live in camps and have worked hard to establish themselves in their adopted country. Some have been given land in remote areas to clear and farm; others work on the mountain roads which need constant maintenance; and, all over India, small groups of Tibetans will be found in the towns, selling clothes.

The man in the background is a Tibetan lama (monk). He is wearing dark crimson robes and turns the prayer wheels inscribed with a mantra (sacred phrase), which Tibetan Buddhists say as many times a day as they can, to keep their minds on God, rather than occupied by distracting thoughts.

Poverty and Agricultural Reform

Poverty in India is a fact of life which cannot be dismissed. Over the last fifty years, however, great efforts have been made by a number of individuals and increasingly by the Government, to find ways of providing basic necessities for everyone.

In 1951 the *Bhoodan* (gift of land) movement was started by Vinoba Bhave, a disciple of Gandhi, to find land for some of the millions of landless labourers. He walked over 50,000 miles, giving talks and asking for donations from the relatively wealthy landowners. He received over four million acres and, although much of this land was marginal and difficult to cultivate, he managed to initiate a change in people's ideas which may lead to a more co-operative way of life. *Bhoodan* was later extended to *Gramadan* (gift of village), so that ownership of land was given to the village as a whole. *Gramadan* has been accepted by over 5000 villages and Bhave's work was continued by Jayaprakash Narayan.

The Government is attempting to help the poor by introducing new laws which give tenants some legal protection. There are Government-run ration shops all over India, which provide a certain amount of food and kerosene to cardholders for a fixed price, and many community development programmes have been set up, offering financial and technical assistance to help villagers carry out projects they feel would be useful, in areas such as primary health care and adult education.

Mahatma Gandhi said:

Everyone, whether he knows it or not, is a thief. Whoever possesses something he does not need is a thief . . . . The one who is rich possesses many superfluous things. If everyone had only what was necessary, nobody would be in need of anything, and all would be satisfied.

In spite of these reforms, the peasant farmer is often troubled by debts, having few resources to carry him over a bad year. Although the system of bonded labour was abolished by law in 1976, it still exists and people who borrow money which is impossible for them to repay, pledge to work entirely for the creditor, receiving nominal wages until the loan is considered repaid. Debts can be carried over from father to son, so some children have to start their working lives as bonded labourers.

Industrial Development

In its endeavour to eradicate poverty, the Government stresses the importance of industrial development. India has important mineral deposits which are being exploited by a combination of state and private enterprise. Whole new towns have been created for the workers at several large industrial projects, such as the steel towns of Bhilai and Bokaro.

Attempts are being made to balance large and small-scale industries and to distribute them around the country so that new opportunities are open to as many people as possible. It is a difficult task and the Government has been criticized for the inefficiency

---

PROMOTING VILLAGE INDUSTRIES

Two important organizations have been set up to promote small-scale and rural industries. One of these is the Khadi and Village Industries Board, which gives information, marketing assistance and sometimes grants to people in cottage industries such as handspinning and weaving (*khadi*), beekeeping and tanning leather. The other organization is the Handicrafts Board, which attempts to improve and market the products of craftsmen all over India. It was originally created by Central Government; now, the different State Governments have set up similar organizations, with their own shops as outlets for the goods.

of most nationalized industries and for spending too much on prestigious capital-intensive projects.

India produces a wide range of manufactured goods, including most of its own bicycles and motor vehicles, textiles and power-generating units. After the U.S.A. and the Soviet Union, India has more trained technicians and engineers than anywhere else and is now able to offer technical assistance to other developing countries.

This blacksmith's forge is a great contrast to the ▷ modern industrial projects being set up in India. It is, however, a much more usual working situation and the blacksmith is assisted by members of his family.

June

June is an extremely hot and oppressive month almost everywhere in India. The dark grey storm clouds are rolling overhead and everybody is waiting for the rain which will come as a welcome relief. Soon after the rain starts, some crops, such as rice, millet and sesame, will be planted, to be harvested in November or December. Jute and cotton are also planted at this time, but take longer to mature. The other main planting season is at the end of the monsoon in September, when wheat, barley, pulses and mustard are planted, to be harvested the following March or April.

The Railways

India's first passenger train ran from Bombay to Thana, a 20-mile journey, in 1853 and by 1880 all the major cities were connected. India's railway system is now the fourth largest in the world and carries over 8 million passengers every day. It provides a very efficient, although overburdened service, which contrasts with the apparent chaos encountered at the station.

When going on a journey, many people just go to the station and camp there until a suitable train is ready to leave. There is always an enormous amount of luggage, which includes bulky bedrolls, water carriers, pots and pans besides a variety of bundles tied up in lengths of cloth. The unreserved coaches are always completely full, people wedged over and under each other, occupying every inch of available space. The more daring take refuge on the roof, although this can be a dangerous way of travelling.

It is possible to reserve a seat or bunk for a small extra charge, although reservations have to be made well in advance, as everything is likely to be booked at least ten days

Buses, too, are generally overcrowded, but most people manage to squeeze in somewhere or wait for the next one. The more athletic manage to climb in through the windows, to make sure of a seat.

Pavement artist. The finished picture will be bright with the colours of many different chalks. Millions of people, who would otherwise be unemployed, set themselves up in business, for example as shoeshiners, barbers, musicians and hawkers, and provide a great variety of services for those who can afford them.

▽

ahead. The journey is then quite comfortable. There are long stops at stations, plenty of time to get out of the train and perhaps have a cup of tea, which, in Northern India, is usually served in handleless, unglazed cups which are thrown away after use. On the train, there is no shortage of food, as many people come into the compartments selling different snacks such as peanuts or split peas roasted with spices and served with a squeeze of lime juice, or samosas, triangular cases of wafer-thin pastry stuffed with spiced vegetables and deep-fried. Meals can be ordered, a choice of vegetarian or meat, and at the next station these miraculously appear in front of you. Small boys come along the train at intervals, with handleless brooms, and energetically, but rather ineffectively, sweep under the seats for a small sum. Singers, often handicapped in

some way, wail plaintive songs to distract you on the journey, hoping to collect a few *paisa* for their efforts, and some beggars may also manage to get on and collect a little money.

Almost all Indians are very interested in foreigners and most are extraordinarily kind and hospitable. On a train journey someone in the carriage is usually able to speak some English and, after a while, will ask a lot of questions about your country, job, salary and purpose of your visit to India. It is quite acceptable for you to ask very direct personal questions back and if the person does not wish to give an exact reply, a rather vague approximation of the truth is much preferred to a direct rebuff. Indians take a lot of time and trouble to help you enjoy their country and by the end of the journey you will often have genuine invitations to stay with people in their homes.

Rath Yatra

In Puri, Orissa, one of the greatest festivals in the whole of India takes place at the end of June. It is known as the Rath Yatra, which means procession of chariots, and is held in honour of Jagannath, Lord of the Universe. Pilgrims from all over the country

---

INDIAN WORDS IN THE ENGLISH LANGUAGE

A number of words have been incorporated into the English language as a result of Britain's contact with India. Examples are:

BUNGALOW — from the words for Bengali house.
CASHMERE — the very fine wool of a mountain goat from Kashmir.
JODHPURS — from trousers commonly worn in North India and taking their name from the town of Jodhpur in Rajasthan.
JUGGERNAUT — from the great *rath* of Jagannath, under the wheels of which devotees used to throw themselves as a sacrifice.
THUG — originally a member of a religious sect that robbed and murdered travellers in parts of northern India during the eighteenth century.

Beach scene.

△
Adivasi woman, Tamil Nadu. Her ear was first pierced when she was a small child and the lobe has gradually stretched with the weight of larger and larger earrings.

◁ *Crowds at Rath Yatra, Puri.*

come for the festival, as Puri is considered to be one of the holiest places in India. Since all the sacred rivers end in the sea, it is also considered purifying and on Puri's long, sandy beach many people go into the water fully clothed for a ritual bathe. They are usually aided by priests and professional helpers, as the waves here are often rough.

The main event of the festival is the procession of three huge *raths* or chariots, each about 14 metres high. The first *rath* carries the image of Lord Jagannath, accompanied by more than 50 priests carrying out the necessary rituals. The other two take his

brother and sister. The *raths* are on great wheels, at least 2 metres in diameter, and are pulled from the temple by thousands of devout pilgrims, down the widest road in Puri to the god's garden house, where the images stay for a week before returning to the temple.

Adivasis

There are still over 40 million tribal people known as *Adivasis* living in India. They are descendants of the original inhabitants of the subcontinent who have been pushed further and further back into the least fertile areas by the dominant Aryans. They are now concentrated in the central jungles of Madhya Pradesh and Orissa and in the mountains of the north eastern states such as Assam. Some of these people still live very close to nature, practising shifting cultivation, where they burn down some of the jungle, work the land for a few years until it is exhausted and then move on to another place. It is a wasteful method of cultivation and difficult to continue in an over-populated country, and so many have to go away and work as forest labourers, on the roads, or for wealthy landowners, for minimal pay. Although the *Adivasis* now have some Government protection and there are still some autonomous communities preserving their tribal heritage, the majority form the most oppressed section of Indian society.

Wildlife

India has a great variety of wildlife. Many animals, particularly the large ones, have suffered, because their habitats have been greatly reduced by the destruction of the jungle and also because of indiscriminate killing for skins and horns. Hunting was a favourite pastime of Indian princes and British army officers, who eventually created

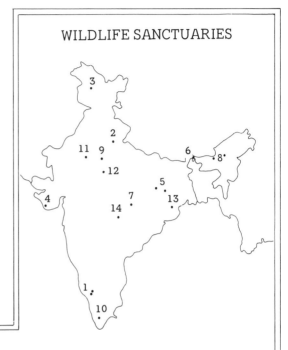

WILDLIFE SANCTUARIES

	NAME	STATE	ANIMALS MOST FREQUENTLY SEEN
1.	Bandipur and Mudumalai	Karnataka and Tamil Nadu	Elephant, wild oxen, leopard, deer, giant squirrel.
2.	Corbett	Uttar Pradesh	Elephant, leopard, bear, deer, birds.
3.	Dachigam	Kashmir	Black and brown bears, Kashmiri stag.
4.	Gir	Gujarat	Asiatic lion. (Gir is now their only home.)
5.	Hazaribagh and Palamau	Bihar	Tiger, leopard, wild oxen, elephant, deer, pig.
6.	Jaldapara	Bengal	Elephant, one-horned rhinoceros, birds.
7.	Kanha	Madhya Pradesh	Tiger, wild oxen, deer.
8.	Kaziranga and Manas	Assam	One-horned rhinoceros, elephant, tiger, wild buffalo, birds.
9.	Keoladeo Ghana	Rajasthan	Water bird sanctuary.
10.	Periyar	Kerala	Elephant, wild oxen, deer, otter, monkeys, birds.
11.	Sariska	Rajasthan	Tiger, leopard, deer, pig.
12.	Shivpuri	Madhya Pradesh	Deer.
13.	Simlipal	Orissa	Elephant, tiger, leopard, deer.
14.	Taroba	Maharashtra	Wild oxen, tiger, leopard, deer, pig, monkeys.

reserves where hunting was permitted only at certain times of the year, so that the number of animals would be kept up and their sport protected. These sanctuaries were taken over and have been enlarged by the Indian Government and are an important tourist attraction.

Early-morning jungle treks at Mudumalai wildlife sanctuary, Tamil Nadu, are popular with Indian and foreign tourists. In the background is a herd of wild elephants. The mahout *(elephant driver) directs the elephant by rubbing his feet behind its ears.*

July

July is a month of rain over most of India. Ideally, it will rain heavily at the end of June and during July, then continue more gently until September. In bad years, the monsoon may finish early, arrive late or not come at all, so there is a drought; or, occasionally, it continues raining very heavily in August and September, causing floods. The monsoon is extremely important to the agricultural communities of India, which account for more than three quarters of the population, and it determines their prosperity, or lack of it, for the following year.

The rainy season is the most unhealthy time of the year, as water supplies often become infected, so that many people suffer

AVERAGE DAYTIME TEMPERATURES AND RAINFALL							
JANUARY	Bombay	Calcutta	Darjeeling	Delhi	Madras	Nagpur	Srinagar
Temperature °C	28	26	7	21	30	23	2
Rainfall mm	3	10	13	3	76	3	38
APRIL							
Temperature °C	32	36	16	36	35	35	13
Rainfall mm	—	44	102	8	16	7	97
JULY							
Temperature °C	30	32	20	36	36	32	22
Rainfall mm	635	330	863	205	102	178	62
OCTOBER							
Temperature °C	31	32	17	33	32	33	12
Rainfall mm	62	114	138	10	310	13	30

◁ *The Taj Mahal in Agra is probably the most beautiful and best-known tomb in the world. It was started in 1632 A.D., as a tribute by the Moghul emperor Shah Jehan, to his wife, Empress Arjumand Banu Begum, who was known as Mumtaz Mahal — the chosen one of the palace. The Sikh and his wife in the foreground are tourists. She is wearing a Punjabi suit, usually worn by women in North Western India. It is made up of shalwar (very full trousers that narrow towards the ankle), kameez (a knee-length tunic or dress) and dupatta (a long scarf of fine chiffon). The man on the right is a professional photographer.*

from gastric complaints and other diseases of insanitation. In some areas, malaria is also common, in spite of widespread eradication programmes; and, although it is still warm the rain makes life difficult for those without adequate shelter and many people get bad coughs.

Islam in India

In spite of Partition, which has meant that most Muslims of the subcontinent now live in Pakistan and Bangladesh, 10% of the Indian population follow Islam, making

INLAID MARBLE

Marble inlay work is done with slivers of semi-precious stones cut very precisely into the marble to make patterns in contrasting colours. There are many workshops in Agra where people still painstakingly do this work, the inlaid marble being used mainly for small decorative boxes and trays.

Islam in India has been very influenced by the Sufis, a mystical sect, and there are many tombs of Sufi saints and poets which are regarded as holy places. This woman wearing a burqa *is in Delhi, at the tomb of Nizamuddin, a Sufi saint who lived during the sixteenth century. Patterns and phrases written in Arabic are generally used as decorations, because Orthodox Muslims are not supposed to depict living beings.*

India the third largest Muslim country in the world, after Indonesia and Bangladesh.

Although Hindu and Muslim communities usually live quite separately, Islam has still had a strong influence on Indian life in general, particularly in the North. The most obvious effects can be seen in the architecture. Cities such as Delhi, Agra and Ahmedabad have many features of Middle Eastern building such as the domes on mosques and tombs, and the huge forts and formal gardens. Decorating them are beautiful tiles, intricate screens and marble inlay work. Islamic customs have also spread; for example, some high caste Hindu women, as well as Muslim, are in *purdah*, which means that no one except their immediate family may see them unless they are completely covered.

The Islamic Calendar

The Islamic calendar is a lunar one and is not adjusted to keep in line with the seasons. As the Islamic year has only 354 days, each of its months falls a little earlier each year, according to the seasons and the Gregorian calendar. In 1982 A.D., Ramadan, the Muslim month of fasting, and Id-ul-Fitr, the big festival which follows it, fell in July.

The Pillars of Islam

There are five duties which all Muslims should carry out, and these are known as the Pillars of Islam. Islam's most fundamental belief is the unity of God. Every time a Muslim prays, he expresses this with the words "There is no god but the One God (known as Allah) and Mohammed is His prophet". This phrase is called the *Shahada*. Mohammed is considered to be the last and greatest of a long line of prophets, which include Moses and Jesus Christ; and Islam is considered the universal religion which supersedes Judaism and Christianity. The Koran is the Muslims' holy book, and is a collection of the divine revelations received

42

by Mohammed on different occasions during his life. The final text was completed within twenty years of his death in 632 A.D., or year 10 of the Islamic calendar, and has never been changed. Every Muslim learns to recite passages from the Koran in Arabic, the language in which it was written.

The most important of a Muslim's regular duties is prayer. The word "Islam" means "submission", and prayer is regarded as the best way to accept and stay in touch with God's will. Five times a day, at sunrise, midday, early afternoon, at sunset and before going to bed, the muezzin or announcer calls people to prayer, usually aided by loudspeakers, from a minaret of the mosque. Muslims everywhere face Mecca, the city in Arabia where Mohammed was born, and intone their prayers, accompanying them with a series of movements known as a *rakah* or bow. Prayers are usually said wherever you happen to be, but, if possible, you go to the mosque where everyone stands in rows behind the *imam* or prayer-leader. Most people attend the mosque at midday on Friday, when the main service of the week is held, at which a preacher gives a long sermon.

The third of a Muslim's obligations is charity. Some money, known as the *Zakat*, which is usually 1/40th of a man's income, is paid to help the poor in addition to other voluntary contributions. Perhaps extending their duty of charity, Muslims are often overwhelmingly hospitable.

The fourth Pillar of Islam is an annual fast. All adult Muslims, except those who are travelling or very ill, must not eat or drink anything between sunrise and sunset during the ninth lunar month, called Ramadan. During Ramadan, people usually get up very early and have a meal before dawn breaks, then

Id celebrations at Jama Masjid, the biggest mosque in Delhi.

BIRIANI

Biriani is a very rich, rice dish which is eaten on special occasions. It originally came from the Middle East and became popular in India during the rule of the Moghuls.

INGREDIENTS

1 tablespoon coriander seeds
1 teaspoon cumin seeds
1 teaspoon fennel seeds } crushed
1 oz fresh ginger
1 teaspoon black pepper
½ teaspoon ground turmeric
2 tablespoons poppy seeds
Juice of 1 lime or ½ lemon
3 cloves
2 inch stick cinnamon
4 cardamoms, crushed
2 cloves garlic
salt and ground black pepper

1 lb lamb
12 oz long grain rice
¹/₃ pint ghee or clarified butter
½ pint curds or yoghurt
2 onions
1 lb small potatoes (parboiled)
½ lb shelled peas
4 tablespoons ground almonds
4-6 shallots
4 oz sultanas
2 oz blanched almonds
2 pints boiling water

Sweetmaker. He is making jalebis, *a very popular sweet in North India. A batter of flour and curd is dropped in spirals into the hot oil and deep-fried until golden. They are served covered in syrup. Many Indian sweets are made from milk which has been gently simmered for several hours and stirred constantly until a thick residue remains. These milk-based sweets are always very rich, like the* gulab jamuns *in the dish at the front on the right. Balls of solid condensed milk are deep-fried and then soaked in rose-scented syrup.*

METHOD

Wash the rice and soak it in plenty of water for about 1 hour. Wash and dry the meat. Cut it into cubes and cover with the crushed spices mixed with lime juice. Put the meat in a saucepan with salt, cloves, cinnamon and cardamoms. Add the curds, cover and cook gently for about 1 hour. While the meat is cooking, heat some ghee in another pan and fry the onions until soft but not brown. Add the drained rice and crushed garlic. Season with salt and pepper. Cook gently, stirring all the time until the rice is translucent. Add water and boil for 10 minutes. Drain the rice and add to the meat with ground almonds, parboiled potatoes and peas. Simmer for about 20 minutes. In a separate pan fry the shallots in ghee until crisp. Remove them, then toss the sultanas and blanched almonds in ghee until lightly roasted.

To serve, remove cloves, cinnamon and cardamoms. Place the biriani on a heated dish garnished with shallots, sultanas and almonds.

eat again after nightfall. Muslims also have a general dietary restriction and may not eat pork or drink alcohol. When the new moon is just visible immediately after Ramadan, there is one of the main celebrations of the Muslim year, Id-ul-Fitr. It is a holiday, and so all Muslim shops and businesses are closed and the day is spent with relatives and friends. Presents, very often of new clothes and sweets, are exchanged, many sheep or goats are killed and especially good food is enjoyed by everybody. There is an important service at the mosque, which on this day is packed with crowds of people.

The last duty is the Hajj or pilgrimage to Mecca. If he can possibly afford it, a Muslim must make the Hajj at least once in his life-time. In the twelfth lunar month of the Islamic calendar (October in 1982) Muslims from all over the world congregate in Mecca and take part in a series of ceremonies. When they return home, people who have made the journey are regarded with great respect and are known as Hajjis.

August

For most of India, August is another month of rain. Kashmir, however, receives most of its rain in March and April and it is now harvest time here. Wheat and barley are being cut and threshed, and all the temperate fruits grown in Kashmir, such as apricots, apples and grapes, are ripe. Much of the fruit and nuts, such as almonds and walnuts, are sent down to the cities on the plains.

Amarnath Yatra

The Amarnath cave, high in the mountains about 70 miles from Pahalgam, is the destination for thousands of pilgrims this month. They make a very arduous trek to see a great pillar of ice which reaches its fullest height of about eight feet, about the time of the August full moon. The ice pillar is regarded as a *lingam*, the symbol of the god Shiva who is said to have taught Parvati, his wife, the secrets of the universe here. The cave is, therefore, regarded as a very sacred place and devotees of Shiva come here each year from all over India.

Pilgrimage

From time immemorial, pilgrimage has been considered an important means of spiritual regeneration. There are thousands of sacred places all around India, where people go on pilgrimages. In the North, the most important are Amarnath, Badrinath and Kedarnath; in the South, Rameswaram and Kanya Kumari; in the West, Dwarka; in the East, Puri, and in the centre, Varanasi, Allahabad and Mathura. All over the country there are *dharmsalas*, usually built by wealthy people as an act of charity, where pilgrims can stay, for a very small charge. Most pilgrims have little expectation of comfort, so a place to lie down, wash and cook is all that is needed. Indians generally do not regard privacy as necessary or even desirable, far preferring the company of others so that life can be enjoyed together.

Sadhus

Great importance is attached to the spirit

in India, and so society allows many people to concentrate on their inner life, without making any material contribution. Householders consider it their duty to give food to *sadhus* (wandering holy men) and feel that, by doing so, they will gain some merit. There are thousands of *sadhus* in India, usually scantily dressed in orange, with beads round their necks and their bodies smeared with ash. *Shaivite babas*, followers of Shiva, have three horizontal white lines across their foreheads and long matted ringlets of hair and carry a trident, while those *sadhus* who follow Vishnu have a white "U" marked on their foreheads with a long vertical stripe of bright red in the middle of it.

Sadhus have renounced the usual worldly pursuits, to devote themselves to spiritual practices. Most of their lives are spent travelling, as, traditionally, they are not supposed to spend more than a few days in the same place nor keep more food or money than will sustain them for a short time. They often undergo self-imposed mortifications of the flesh, such as fasting, remaining immobile in an awkward position for long periods, or piercing their cheeks with skewers, in an attempt to have mystical experiences and know God. Many *sadhus* make a circuit of sacred places every few years and, from time to time, visit their *gurus*. *Guru* means "teacher" and, traditionally, an aspirant has to work long and hard before a *guru* will accept him as a disciple, for it is important that the *guru* be sure of the other's character before imparting knowledge that will give him

Two sadhus and all their belongings. The brass pots they are carrying are for water and are known as lotas.

power that could possibly be used in a destructive way.

At times, the *sadhus* have big gatherings at religious festivals, known as *melas*. The most important is the Kumbha *mela*, which is held every three years at Ujjain, Hardwar, Allahabad and Nasik in turn, so that the *mela* comes once every twelve or thirteen years to each town. Over a million pilgrims also attend the Kumbha *melas*, which involve great feats of organization.

Hardwar and Rishikesh

Hardwar is an ancient city of many temples, and is also known as the Gate of the Ganga, because of its situation at the end of a gorge through which the river rushes out onto the plains. On the *ghats* along the bank of the Ganga are some stones, said to be stamped with Vishnu's footprint, which are the object of great veneration. Rishikesh is a small town a few miles north of Hardwar and another place of pilgrimage. It is surrounded by woods and is also situated on the Ganga, which is very blue and fast-flowing here. The fish in the river are said to be sacred. They are fed regularly by pilgrims and never harmed, so are very tame. The town is full of *ashrams*, including a centre for Transcendental Meditation and Swami Shivananda's *ashram*, both of which have become well-known outside India.

Yoga

Yoga and meditation have become increasingly popular in the West, as ways of relieving the strains of modern life. Hatha yoga, the form that has spread most widely and is most commonly practised outside India, is an ancient system that teaches control of mind and body through physical exercises and breathing techniques. The aim is deep relaxation which frees the mind from distraction so that it can become at one with God.

Transcendental Meditation became popular in the West during the 1960s after the Beatles went to Rishikesh to visit the Maharishi. The two men under the sign are asleep. Most people cover their faces when sleeping outside.

Medicine

Closely connected to yogic philosophy is the *ayurvedic* system of medicine, which follows ancient laws set down in the Vedas. It is a holistic system, in that it regards different parts of the body as being inseparably connected with each other, so that illness arises when the body is out of balance. Remedies are based on naturally occurring substances, such as herbs and finely ground minerals.

The Muslim system of medicine is known as *unani* and its doctors as *hakims*. It is also a holistic system using herbal and mineral remedies.

OIL BATHS

The sun in India is very strong and dries out your hair and skin so much that most people take weekly oil baths. Sesame or mustard oil is massaged into the body and, besides helping the oil penetrate, the massage also relaxes the muscles. Coconut oil is usually used on the hair, and the whole head is massaged to ease tension and help the growth of healthy hair. Different herbs are sometimes added to the oils to improve them. After the oil bath you take an ordinary shower, and just enough oil is left on the hair and skin to keep them smooth without feeling sticky.

Homoeopathic medicine is widely practised in India. Homoeopaths try to aid the body's healing processes by using minute amounts of medicine which, in large quantities, cause the very symptoms that are being experienced.

It is a status symbol in India to bottle-feed your baby. It can be dangerous, however, as it is often difficult to keep bottles sterile and the reconstituted milk quickly turns sour in the heat. Also pure water is not always available and the expense of the milk powder leads people to use too little of it, so that the milk is very dilute.

Allopathic (Western) medicine is increasingly important and has done much to point out the significance of germs and how to prevent them spreading. Vaccination has helped prevent widespread epidemics of smallpox, cholera and typhoid — which is one reason for the increase in life expectancy. Problems are often encountered, however, in that many people do not understand how harmful modern drugs can be if not taken according to specific instructions and, as the medicines are very expensive, people tend not to take a full course of treatment and this allows a secondary and often more serious infection to break out. Unscrupulous drug companies have taken advantage of the lack of stringent controls in India, to sell off drugs that have been prohibited in the West, because of their side effects or because they are out-of-date.

Janmashtami

An important festival for many people this month is Janmashtami — the celebration of Lord Krishna's birthday. Krishna is an incarnation of Vishnu the Creator and is believed to be the divine author of the *Bhagavad Gita*, the most important book of the epic poem *Mahabharata*. He is one of the most popular gods, generally associated with the devotional side of Hinduism. There are many legends about him and he has inspired many creative people — artists, poets, musicians and dancers. At Janmash-

Gentleness in a baby food

Vijayaspray
Superior Milk Food For Babies

Vijayaspray
The answer to a mother's prayer

tami, all over India and especially at Mathura and Brindavan in Uttar Pradesh, where Krishna was born and spent his childhood, there are plays depicting episodes of his life. The night is spent singing devotional songs and chanting prayers.

Pictures of the gods (Radha and Krishna on the left and Vishnu on the right) are frequently used as trademarks for many kinds of goods, in particular, beedis, small cheap cigarettes.

Ganesh Chaturthi

Ganesh is the elephant-headed god, Shiva's son. He is the god of wisdom and good fortune and is invoked before any prayer, as he is known to grant boons or favours. Ganesh Chaturthi is an important festival in Maharashtra, where huge clay models of him are taken out on floats and followed by a great procession which includes a lot of music-making, singing, drumming, blowing conches — huge shells — and clashing cymbals. The procession goes to the sea or to a lake and Ganesh is immersed in the water before returning.

Rolling beedis. A small amount of tobacco is wrapped in a leaf and then secured with a twist of cotton thread.

49

September

Kerala

Kerala is a beautiful state; it is lush and green and known as the land of coconuts, as its long coastline is fringed with palm trees. Inland, in the cooler climate of the hills, tea, coffee and many spices are grown. There are also stands (groups) of tall, slender areca palms, which give a nut that is cut up and chewed with a peppery leaf and a little lime paste. This combination is known as *paan*, and chewing it produces lots of bright red juice which you spit out, leaving your mouth tingling and refreshed.

Rice is the main crop grown in Kerala and is eaten at every meal, although in different forms. *Iddlis* are steamed cakes made of ground rice, which are often eaten for breakfast. They are very light and accompanied by spicy coconut chutney. Lunch is the main meal of the day and your plate is usually a disposable one, being a large piece of banana leaf. The leaf is first sprinkled with water and wiped clean; then a huge pile of rice is heaped in the middle of it. Behind the rice are small amounts of at least two different curries, several chutneys and pickles, a small bowl of curd, a pappadum and perhaps some banana chips. *Sambhar*, a tangy lentil soup, is poured over the rice, and as the food is very runny in South India, you use the whole of the right hand to squeeze the rice and some of the side dishes into a ball which you flick into your mouth with your thumb. The meal ends with some more rice which is mixed with the curd and a little salt. The evening meal is often *dosa*, pancakes made of ground rice, and small black beans. The *dosa* are accompanied by fresh chutney and *sambhar*, and are sometimes filled with spiced vegetables.

Keralans generally reach a much higher level of education than people in other parts of India and have the highest rate of literacy in the country (70% as opposed to the national average of 36%). Education in India is free up to the age of fourteen, but parents have to provide their children with school materials. Sometimes extra help with the work at home is needed, so that, although

◁ Green coconuts for sale. The top is sliced off with a large knife and the watery juice is deliciously cool and thirst-quenching. If the coconut is allowed to ripen and go brown, a thick white layer is formed inside the nut. This is grated and a little water added so that the coconut milk or cream can be extracted. It is used in many South Indian dishes. If the white coconut meat is dried, it is known as copra and used to make oil. The coconut is surrounded by a very thick fibrous husk which is removed. The coarse fibres, known as coir, are used to make rope, matting and doormats.

SPICES

CARDAMOM (*elachi*): small green pods containing about twelve seeds which are very aromatic when crushed. They are a common ingredient in curry powders but are also widely used to flavour sweets, puddings and tea. They are sometimes chewed after meals as an aid to digestion and a breath freshener.

CHILLI (*mirchi*): small red or green peppers. They are used fresh or dry to give the hot taste in curries and pickles.

CINNAMON (*dalchini*): the fragrant inner bark of a tree which is used in both sweet and savoury dishes.

CLOVES (*laung*): dried buds from a tree which are strongly flavoured and used in curries as well as puddings.

CORIANDER (*dhania*): a relative of parsley. The fresh leaves are pleasantly aromatic and used in many savoury dishes. The seeds are usually lightly roasted and used in most curries.

CUMIN (*jeera*): distinctively flavoured, long, brown seeds used in most curries.

CURRY LEAVES (*kari patta*): leaves of a small tree which are used in many South Indian savoury dishes.

FENNEL (*sawnf*): long green seeds tasting of aniseed. They are used in some curries and are eaten after meals as a digestive aid and breath freshener.

FENUGREEK (*methi*): the aromatic leaves are eaten as a vegetable. The seeds are lightly roasted and occasionally used in curries.

GINGER (*adruk*): the rhizome is used in many dishes and gives a pleasant, slightly hot taste. .

MUSTARD SEEDS (*rai*): small black seeds which are fried and added to many savoury dishes.

PEPPER (*kali mirch*): peppercorns are the dried berries of a vine. Black pepper is used in most savoury dishes.

POPPY SEEDS (*khus khus*): tiny white or grey seeds used to thicken the sauce in many curries.

TAMARIND (*imli*): the ripe pod is soaked in water and used to give the slightly acid flavour to many South Indian dishes such as *sambhar*.

TURMERIC (*haldi*): a dried root which gives a bright yellow colour as well as flavour to curries and rice dishes.

Girl fetching water from a tap that is used by many ▷ households. The water is clean and safe to drink. Painted on the wall are red flags with the hammer and sickle, symbol of one of the Keralan Communist parties.

education is regarded very highly, many children from poor families do not attend school. Education is generally very formal, but the Government has recently introduced a new syllabus for the whole country which places more emphasis on vocational training for cottage industries and handicrafts. In most parts of the country, school is attended in shifts, either morning or afternoon, as there are too many pupils for available teachers and space. Christian missions are very involved in education and their schools are mainly attended by children from comparatively wealthy families, although not necessarily Christian.

Politics are an important part of life in Kerala and the state was one of the first places in the world freely to elect a Communist Government. Red flags are seen everywhere. Unions are well-organized and there are many strikes. Kerala appears very tranquil, but it is the most densely populated state in India and there is much unemployment and social unrest. Because they are well-educated and ambitious, many Keralans have emigrated to East Africa or work in the Middle East.

Onam

At the end of August, everyone in Kerala spring-cleans and paints their house, also carrying out any repairs that are necessary after the rainy season. This is done in preparation for Keralan New Year, which is celebrated about a week before the most important festival of the year here, Onam.

Onam celebrates the return of a legendary king called Mahabali. Under his rule, the people of Kerala prospered, but he was defeated in battle by one of the gods. However Mahabali was allowed to return to his kingdom once a year and visit his subjects. To welcome him, women make huge designs with all kinds of flowers. They also draw intricate *rangoli* patterns on the ground, with a paste of rice flour, and surround them with small clay pyramids and oil lamps. The festival lasts four days; greetings cards and presents, usually of new clothes, are exchanged and employers give their workers an Onam bonus. Food is prepared with extra care and a special vegetable dish is made, called *avial*, in which all the vegetables are either green or white. *Avial* is very rich and quite sweet, from all the coconut cream that is added, and it forms part of the festive rice plate eaten for lunch, which can include more than twenty different dishes.

A few days after Onam, races of huge "snake-boats" are held at several different places on the inland waterways, which are swollen now after the rains. The banks are crowded with people, many stand in the river and others climb trees, hoping for a better view. After a few practice runs, the races begin.

Cochin

Cochin, on the coast of Kerala, has a very interesting history as, through the ages, people from many different parts of the world have come here and left their mark. The Jews first came to Kerala in the sixth century B.C. and many followed 700 years later, fleeing from persecution by the Romans who ruled Jerusalem. The Jewish community is now very small, but there is still a synagogue in Cochin and part of the

RANGOLI

In South India, women draw out complicated patterns on the ground outside their houses in the early morning. There are many different designs, all of which have a special significance appropriate on different occasions. A small roller with holes, that allow white powder to trickle out, is sometimes used, or the design is drawn freehand with a mixture of rice flour and water. On special occasions coloured powders are also used. This *rangoli* shows a lotus flower, a kind of waterlily, which represents beauty and purity.

△
Practice runs leading up to the snake-boat races. Each boat comes from a different village and is paddled by about 100 men. In the middle of the boat, several men stand under a colourful parasol and act as cheerleaders for the oarsmen, keeping them in rhythm with each other.

city is called Jew Town. Many Keralans are Christians and, in 1510, the Portuguese built the first European church in India here. Before his body was taken back to Portugal in 1538, the great explorer, Vasco da Gama,

There are many of these Chinese fishing nets in Cochin, but they are not to be seen anywhere else in India. They are levered up and down every few minutes and a small pile of fish is removed from the middle of the net. Most fishing in India is done from small boats, many of which are more like rafts than the fairly sturdy craft in this photograph. There are fishing villages all along the Keralan coast and they usually work as a collective — that is, the value of the catch is divided between all those who took part, after setting aside one share for the replacement of equipment. The fishermen's wives take away some of the fish and a middleman usually auctions the rest to merchants who come out to the village to buy for nearby makets. ▷

53

Cochin is made up of several islands which are connected to the town of Ernakulam on the mainland by ferries. Cochin is an important port and there are huge, modern ships in the harbour, alongside dug-out canoes and punts used for local transportation of goods through the extensive backwaters of Kerala. There are also many warehouses to store the goods waiting for transportation — great bundles of rope, chests of tea and sacks of fragrant cardamoms and ginger. The streets are very narrow and congested. Men straining to push hand carts piled high with goods compete for space with rickshaws and pedestrians; and, from time to time, a huge lorry horn blaring, tries to inch its way through the crowd. The lorries are very brightly painted and on top of the cab have signs emblazoned with "Sri Krishna" or "Hail Mary", according to their owner's religious beliefs.

The man on the right has elephantiasis, a disease which is so common around Cochin, that it is sometimes referred to as "Cochin leg".

was buried in the church where his gravestone can still be seen. The Portuguese were followed by the Dutch, who have left several solid buildings as a reminder of their presence, and the Arabs also came, both to trade, particularly for cardamom, the spice they like to add to coffee, and to convert people to Islam.

Effigy of the demon Ravana at the Ram Leela ▷ ground where it will be set alight.

Dusshera

Towards the end of September is the important ten-day festival of Dusshera. It is celebrated in different ways all over India and is known by several different names. Generally, though, Dusshera celebrates the victory of good over evil, represented by different gods and demons in different parts of the country. It is a time of great fun and merrymaking. Houses, motor vehicles and bicycles are decorated with long chains of leaves, coloured flags and many flowers, particularly sweet-smelling jasmine and bright marigolds.

In most of North India, the festival is known as Ram Leela and every village puts on plays, acting out the story of Rama's life, told in the epic poem, the *Ramayana*. Performances last all day and much of the night, the audience being free to come and watch for as long as they are interested and then wander away or doze for a while. This free-and-easy attitude is usual for most concerts and plays, which generally last at least five hours. The festival ends at full moon, when huge effigies of the demon Ravana, who was defeated by Rama, are taken to an open space and set alight. Fire crackers are put in the stuffing of the demon and it soon explodes, to the cheers of the crowds.

Dusshera brings in the new planting season for crops that are sown at the end of the monsoon, such as wheat, barley and pulses.

Rama's name is often used as a greeting in North India. People shout "Jai Ram" (Victory to Rama) or simply "Ram, Ram" to each other as they pass.

October

The Mahatma

Gandhi has become a legendary figure and is particularly remembered on his birthday, 2 October. Generally, birthdays are not celebrated in India after the first year, as they are not considered important and there are so many other festivals to enjoy. Saints' birthdays, though, are often regarded as special days.

The Mahatma, meaning "Great Soul", as Mohandas Karamchand Gandhi became known, was born in 1869 in Porbandar, Gujarat. As a young man, he went to England to study law and, after qualifying, practised in South Africa. He returned to India in 1914 and five years later joined the movement for Home Rule (Independence), after the Jallianwalla Bagh massacre.

Gandhi worked tirelessly for Home Rule and was imprisoned by the British many times. He became famous for his effective, non-violent methods of protest which he called *Satyagraha*, which means the "force of truth". He firmly believed that anything won by violence was not worthwhile. One of the methods he used was a boycott of British goods such as cloth, which he encouraged people to produce themselves in the traditional way. This handspun and handwoven cloth is known as *khadi* and

RABINDRANATH TAGORE

It was Rabindranath Tagore (1861-1941) who first gave Gandhi the title of Mahatma. He is India's best-known poet and was awarded the Nobel Prize for Literature in 1913 for his anthology *Gitanjali (Song Offerings)*, which he translated into English prose from the original in Bengali. He was given a knighthood in 1915 but returned it four years later, after the Jallianwalla Bagh massacre. Tagore firmly believed in the benefits of interaction between people of different races and founded an experimental school and international university at Shanti Niketan in West Bengal.

No. 35 from *Gitanjali*
Where the mind is without fear and the head is held high;
Where knowledge is free;
Where the world has not been broken up into fragments by narrow domestic walls;
Where words come out from the depth of truth;
Where tireless striving stretches its arms towards perfection;
Where the clear stream of reason has not lost its way into the dreary desert sand of dead habit;
Where the mind is led forward by thee into ever-widening thought and action —
Into that heaven of freedom, my Father, let my country awake.

(Macmillan and Co. Limited, St. Martin's Street, London, 1913)

became almost a uniform for the advocates of Home Rule, as did the white Congress caps which are still worn by many men.

Gandhi managed to give popular appeal to what started as a middle-class movement for Home Rule and extended it to the millions in the villages. He initiated many social reforms and, although he was a very devout Hindu, fought hard against caste oppression and religious ritual. He campaigned to improve the lot of the Untouchables, whom he renamed Harijans, or children of God, and also felt that women should have equal rights and education. He was convinced that economic development should come through handicrafts and small-scale technological innovations, encouraging people to stay in their villages which he hoped would once again become relatively self-sufficient communities. This is happening in a very limited

Gandhi is still a well-remembered figure and a ▷ picture of him was used on these posters over 30 years after his death.

Happy Child – Nation's Pride

International Year of the child 1979

◁ *Man decorating pots. A similar style of folk painting is used to decorate people's homes in many parts of India. The small dishes are used for oil lamps, which are set out in rows all over the house at Diwali. Some oil is poured into the dish and a piece of tightly rolled cloth is dipped into it as a wick and lit at the other end.*

way, however, as modern India's hopes for the future rely heavily on industrial development.

Between 1934 and 1946 tensions between Hindus and Muslims increased and there were terrible riots and massacres during the time leading up to Partition. Gandhi pioneered the hunger strike as a means of protest and managed to halt the brutalities. On 30 January 1948, only a few months after Independence, he was assassinated by a Hindu fanatic for his support of Muslims. He was cremated in Delhi where, as a memorial, there is a plain marble slab inscribed with his dying words: "Hai Ram", roughly translated as "Oh Lord".

Diwali

Twenty days after Dusshera comes Diwali, the festival of lights. It is dedicated to Vishnu and his wife Lakshmi, the goddess of prosperity, who is worshipped by many people of the *Vaishya* or merchant caste. In Gujarat, Diwali is also New Year, so Gujaratis clean and paint their houses as Keralans did for their New Year, six weeks ago. Businessmen discard their old account books and start new ones, hoping for good fortune in the year to come. At dusk, hundreds of tiny lamps called *divas* are placed all over the house. Shops and offices are decorated with coloured electric lights, and in the evening there are often fireworks. People enjoy rich sweets and the following day go to visit friends and relatives.

Markets

The housewife can do almost all her shopping

MONEY

One rupee is worth about six British pence (1982) and since decimalization in 1957 has been divided into 100 *paisa*. It is necessary to keep plenty of coins and notes of small denominations, as traders and people offering services, such as rickshaw drivers, are often unable to change a large note. People tend to buy their goods in very small amounts, as they need them, rather than stocking up, and so transactions usually involve only small sums of money. Most traders will not accept torn notes, although they can be changed at a bank. When counting large amounts of money or anything else, the words *lakh* meaning 100,000, and *crore*, 10 million, are used.

at home if she wishes, as a wide variety of goods are brought round by different people carrying huge baskets on their heads or on heavily laden bicycles. They shout or sing their wares as they go round — fruit and vegetables, fish, hardware, flowers. About once a week, though, she or one of the men in the family, often a younger brother, will go to the market as there is more choice there and it is cheaper. Indian markets are always colourful, busy places, with lots of people, noise and long, loud discussions about the price of each item until a sum is mutually agreed.

Tailor's shop. Very few ready-made clothes are available in India. People generally buy their material and then take it to a tailor with a garment similar to the one they want made and the tailor will copy it, altering the size or style as necessary.
▽

◁ *Wealthy girl at a Bombay club.*

important being textiles, and Bombay produces almost half of India's total output.

People have come from all over India to live in Bombay and regard the city as the most progressive in the country. A testimony to its enterprise are the skyscrapers — an unusual sight in India — of which most Bombayites are extremely proud. The green, spacious, residential area of Malabar Hill is the home of the jetset, who have taken over

Bombay is the centre of India's film industry, which is the largest in the world. There are always long queues for cinema seats and, at big cinemas in the cities, you often have to book several days in advance. Cinemas are generally very comfortable and air-conditioned. Musicals are the most popular kind of film and stars are hero-worshipped by their vast audiences. The other poster warns of unscrupulous merchants who add cheap substitutes to foods to make them go further.

▽

Cities

Since Independence there has been a great increase in the number of people living in cities, partly because of economic depression in rural areas and also because of the growing demand for office and industrial workers as the foundation of India's economy changes from agriculture to commerce and industry. This month we shall pay a flying visit to the largest cities in India, Bombay and Calcutta.

Bombay

India's commercial capital is Bombay, which has an excellent harbour, making it one of the largest ports in Asia. It is a centre for many different industries, the most

59

MOTHER TERESA

Mother Teresa was born in 1910 in Skopje, Yugoslavia, of Albanian parents. When she was 17, she entered a convent and soon after went to Darjeeling, in north-eastern India. After she had taken her religious vows, she was sent to Calcutta to teach at a Catholic High School. She stayed there until 1948, when she was given permission by the Pope to start a new order of nuns. She did some medical training and then started work in the *bustees*, teaching the children and offering help and advice to the people who lived there. She soon resolved, however, to try to help the poorest of the poor, those who lived on the city streets, many of whom were overwhelmed by hunger and illness. Other girls soon joined Mother Teresa and they became known as the Missionaries of Charity. In 1952 they obtained a disused building and turned it into a home for dying, destitute people whom the sisters cared for and allowed to die in a peaceful, loving atmosphere or, if possible, nursed back to health. Mother Teresa later set up a home for abandoned children and a centre where lepers could live and receive treatment. As more people have joined the Missionaries of Charity or offered their help as lay co-workers, Mother Teresa's work has spread to many other places in India and since 1965 to other countries too. In 1979, Mother Teresa received international recognition for her work, when she received the Nobel Peace Prize.

the exclusive clubs established by the British and spend their leisure hours swimming, playing golf and bridge or going to the races. For evening entertainment there are many fashionable restaurants and discos. Areas of the city tend to be devoted to a particular community — for example, one caste group or Christians or Parsees — and in any available space tiny shacks are constructed by the poor, from flattened-out tins, matting or pieces of cloth. Many people do not even have a shack as their home and have to live on the pavements.

Calcutta

The largest city in India is Calcutta, built on both sides of the river Hooghly, a channel of the Ganga. Calcutta is sometimes described as a dying city because of its problems of overcrowding and poverty, but it seems to be a very busy trading centre, inhabited by extremely lively, talkative people.

Like Bombay, the central part of the city was designed in the nineteenth century and has some of the best surviving examples of Victorian architecture. Calcutta has also been compared with the industrial cities of Victorian England in which so many people struggled to make ends meet. Industrially, Calcutta is best-known for light engineering and its jute mills, which produce sacks and matting.

At the turn of the century, many people came from the states of Bihar, Uttar Pradesh and Orissa which periodically suffered famine. The *bustees*, great areas of cheap housing in Calcutta, developed as a result of this influx of people. They are legitimate settlements, as people rent the huts, although facilities are minimal. In 1970 the Calcutta Metropolitan Development Authority was created to improve housing conditions, water, sanitation and transport in the city.

Bengal, and Calcutta in particular, is generally acknowledged to be India's most innovative cultural centre and is the home of many well-known writers, artists and musicians.

November

Most of the subcontinent is pleasantly cool and dry during November. In the South and North East, it is harvest time for the rice and millet that were sown at the end of June, when the rains started. In the North West, the wheat, sown at the end of the rainy season, is still green. This month we shall visit Rajasthan or Rajputana — Abode of Kings — as it was called before Independence when it was made up of many separate states ruled by princes. Much of Rajasthan is desert and it is inhabited by a proud, warlike people. Its cities were built with great walls and forts to protect them in the many battles that have been fought here.

Pushkar Mela

Pushkar is a small town in Rajasthan, built on one side of a lake and believed to be a very holy place. Most of Pushkar's inhabitants are Brahmins and the whole town is completely vegetarian, which means that no meat, fish or eggs — that is, foods that involve taking life — may be brought within the town's boundary. There are many temples and *dharmsalas* (pilgrim's hostels) in the town, including the only temple in India to the god Brahma, creator of the Universe.

Once a year, about a week before the full moon at the beginning of November, thousands of people arrive in Pushkar for the *mela* (fair). They have travelled from towns and villages all over Rajasthan, many walking across the desert, bringing their livestock with them.

Pushkar prepares itself for this invasion of people, collecting fodder, firewood and food to sell to the visitors. A city of tents, many times the size of the town, springs up in the

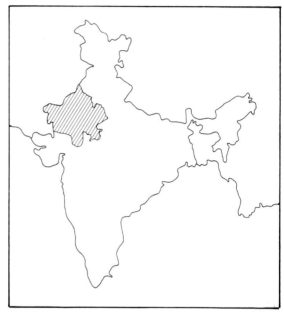

Rajasthan

desert. A fairground appears with a big wheel, make-shift cinemas, sideshows, entertainers such as jugglers, snake charmers and acrobats, besides hundreds of stalls selling an unimaginable variety of goods from pots and pans, to saddles and harnesses, shoes, jewellery and blankets. The *mela* is an opportunity to buy and sell livestock, mainly

MARWARIS

The Marwaris, whose homeland is in Rajasthan, are one of the richest and most influential trading communities in India. They have spread to different parts of the country and many are Jains, renowned for their business acumen and thrift.

camels, bullocks and horses, as well as to obtain goods that are not available at home. The crowds of flamboyantly dressed people offer a great contrast to the barren scenery.

People and their livestock who have come to Pushkar for the mela.

The *mela* is also a religious event, attracting many *sadhus* and beggars too, as people tend to be more generous than usual during festivals. It is considered to be a very auspicious time to bathe in the lake and wash away your sins, and so early in the morning the *ghats* leading down to the water are

Itinerant musician. He wanders around the country playing, singing and telling stories, in return for a little food from the houses he visits. In days before newspapers and the radio, people like this were an important source of news, eagerly received by villagers.

Rajasthani woman peeling a piece of sugarcane which she is going to chew. All Indian women love jewellery and tend to carry their wealth around with them rather than depositing it in a bank. The heavy anklets are silver, some of the bracelets are bone and the nose ring is gold studded with semi-precious stones.

crowded with people performing their purifying rituals.

After the full moon people start on their journeys home, leaving the citizens of Pushkar to clear up after the festivities and its tradesmen to count their money.

Jaipur

The state capital of Rajasthan is Jaipur, whose craftsmen are well-known for their colourfully printed and tie-dyed fabrics, fine painting, and cutting and setting of precious stones. It is a beautiful city built of rose-pink sandstone and was designed by Maharajah Jai Singh in the eighteenth century.

The Maharajah was very interested in science, mathematics and astronomy, in particular. He designed an observatory which was built near the palace, with huge instruments, some of which are about 30 metres high.

Indians generally enjoy having their photograph taken. These two children have been brought to Pushkar for the mela, to beg, as people are more generous than usual at events such as this.

Rajasthani men in a small restaurant after lunch. Their turbans are made from pieces of cloth about 6 metres long and are very bright colours, generally red, pink or yellow, which contrast with their white clothes.

They are remarkably accurate and he later supervised the building of observatories in Delhi, Ujjain and Varanasi.

Science

Many scientific discoveries have been made in India; the most widely used today are algebra and the decimal system of counting which were originally used in calculations for astronomy. They were eventually passed on to Europe via the Arabs. Astrology is closely connected to astronomy and is considered an important science in India. It is the study of how people are influenced by the relative positions of the sun, moon, planets and stars, and astrologers are often consulted before major decisions are made.

India is also proud of its modern scientific achievements and has many scientists of world renown. Atomic and meteorological research are very important, besides new developments for agriculture, such as heavier-yielding strains of cereals which are suited to local conditions.

Guru Nanak Jayanti

Guru Nanak (1469-1539) was the founder of the Sikh religion and taught his followers to worship one God and serve their fellow men. He and the nine *gurus* who followed him are regarded as saintly people through whom the word of God was revealed. The birthdays of all the *gurus* are regarded as holy days, but only those of Guru Nanak and the last *guru*, Gobind Singh, are celebrated as festivals.

Guru Gobind Singh lived in the seventeenth century and, under his direction, most Sikhs joined the martial brotherhood known as the Khalsa, which was formed in reaction to oppression by the Muslim rulers. All members of the Khalsa wear the 5 Ks and men take the name Singh, which means "lion", and women, Kaur, meaning "princess". When Guru Gobind Singh died, he left the Granth, a book of teachings and hymns composed by the Sikh *gurus* and several Hindu and

The Golden Temple at Amritsar is the most important centre for the Sikhs. It was founded in 1579 by the fourth Sikh guru, Ram Das, who constructed the tank (pool) first. The water it contains is said to have miraculous healing powers. The temple buildings surround the sacred tank and many of them are used as a free kitchen and rest-house, as Sikhs offer hospitality to all those who need it.

Muslim saints. The Granth, is considered to be a living spiritual guide and is regarded with great reverence.

Guru Nanak Jayanti is celebrated by taking the Granth from the *gurdwara* (Sikh temple) and putting it on a canopied float decorated with flowers. It leads a great procession round the town or village, during which verses from the holy book are recited. Afterwards, speakers give lectures to the crowds over loudspeakers and music is played by several different bands.

Almost all Sikhs originally come from the Punjab, although they have spread to all parts of India and many have gone abroad. They are known for their self-confidence and are generally very enterprising people who have made the best of opportunities outside their homeland, which is one of the richest parts of India.

December

Christianity

Although Christianity is practised by a very small minority in India, there are over 15 million Christians in the country. Indian Christians say that their religion was brought by the apostle Thomas (known as Doubting Thomas), who landed on the coast of Kerala in 52 A.D., which, they point out, is several years before St Paul arrived in Rome. Today, the largest Christian communities in India are still on the west coast — in Goa, where they are almost entirely Roman Catholic, and in Kerala. The Church in Kerala is very divided and there are many different sects. The main division is between the Syrian and Latin churches who both believe that only they are true to the original Christianity brought by St Thomas. The most obvious difference between the churches is that the Syrian church holds its services in Syro-Chaldaic, a language similar to the Aramaic that Jesus spoke, while in the Roman Catholic church, Latin was used but has now been replaced by the vernacular. Most converts to the Syrian church came from high caste Hindu families, whereas Roman Catholic converts came mainly from the fishermen who are low caste. There are also several Protestant denominations.

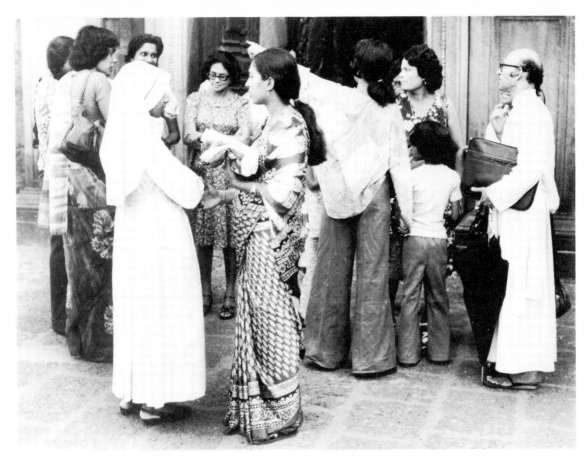

Goa

For Christmas in India we shall go and cele-
brate with the Goans. It is the pleasantest
season of the year here, dry, sunny and
relatively cool. Early on Christmas Eve,
women and children go to the church to put
up decorations. They also recreate the scene
of the nativity, using painted clay figures of
animals, shepherds and the three Kings as
well as Mary, Joseph and the baby Jesus in
the manger. Most people also decorate their
houses with colourful paper lampshades
shaped like stars, fairy lights and sometimes
paperchains. Everyone goes to Mass either
at midnight or in the morning and often
there are nativity plays and carol singing
later in the day. Cards and presents are
exchanged and especially good food is
prepared.

The Portuguese arrived in Goa in the sixteenth century and have greatly influenced

Outside the Basilica of Bom Jesus, the most
important church in Old Goa. St Francis Xavier's
body lies in a silver casket in the Basilica and is
said to be in a remarkable state of preservation.
From time to time it is revealed to the public and
is the object of great veneration. Goans dress in
many different styles; women often wear short
dresses, a very unusual sight in other parts of India.

life there. St Francis Xavier came in 1542
and a great city, Old Goa, was built, about
10 miles from the modern capital of Panaji.
The site proved to be unhealthy, however,
and now there is little left of it except for
the huge churches built round a central
square which continue to be a place of
pilgrimage.

Although the countryside is no different
from surrounding Maharashtra and Karna-
taka, the atmosphere of Goa is unique. Goans
are known for their gaiety and are usually

CASHEWS

The Portuguese introduced cashew trees from South America in the sixteenth century, as a good crop to bind the thin, sandy soils on the coast. Goa is covered with the low, spreading trees, which now provide one of India's most important sources of foreign exchange, as all the best-quality nuts are exported. The cashew tree begins to bear 3 or 4 years after planting and the main harvest is in March and April. At the moment, the trees are in flower. A kidney-shaped nut is produced, attached at the base of a fragrant fruit called a cashew apple which can be eaten raw or is used to make *feni*, a popular Goan alcoholic drink. The nut is surrounded by a thick shell which contains a corrosive oil that has to be roasted out before the kernels are extracted for market. India has a large cashew-processing industry and raw nuts are also imported from East Africa to be processed here.

Tamil village near Auroville. The trees provide shade for the small houses which are thatched with palm leaves.

very sociable, gathering in cafés and bars for long talks and a drink. Everyone likes music and singing, the style of which has been strongly influenced by the Portuguese, and, unlike in most of India, alcohol is easily available, of good quality and relatively cheap. Inter-marriage with the Portuguese was common and Goans have adopted many European customs as well as names like de Souza and Fernandez.

After Independence, India asked for Goa to be incorporated into the Republic, but Portugal refused. In 1961, Indian troops occupied Goa, forcing the Portuguese to give up their territories.

Pondicherry

Before leaving India, we shall visit Pondicherry in the South East. It was the most important territory in the subcontinent held by the French and was founded as a trading centre in 1672. Pondicherry was retained until 1954, when it merged into the Republic of India as a union territory, as Goa later became.

Today the town still has obvious French influences which mainly appear through the

architecture. Most of the French residents
have left and few people can speak French,
which has been replaced by English as the
first European language learnt.

The most important institution in the
town is the large *ashram*, which grew up
around Sri Aurobindo Ghose, a poet and
mystic who originally came from Bengal.
For many years the ashram was adminis-
tered by a French woman known simply as
the Mother. The ashram reflects a blend of
Eastern and Western cultures, through the
many activities in which it is involved, such
as bakeries, craft workshops, gardens, publishing and printing, medical services, sports
and education.

Auroville

A few miles outside the town of Pondicherry
is the international community, Auroville,
which was envisaged by the Mother in 1963
as a city of light — that is, a place where
people from all over the world could live and
work together, attempting to perfect themselves according to the spiritual principles
taught by Sri Aurobindo and the Mother. At
present, Auroville is composed of several
small communities interspersed with the
original Tamil villages, which surround the
Matrimandir, its focal point.

*The Matrimandir at Auroville is envisaged as a
golden globe in its final form and will be surrounded
by twelve different gardens. In the foreground is the
monument built for Auroville's foundation day in
1968.*

Books for Further Reading

A Concise History of India by Francis Watson (Thames and Hudson, 1979)
My Village, My Life — Nanpur: A Portrait of an Indian Village by Prafulla Mohanti (Davis Poynter, London, 1973)
Portrait of India by Ved Mehta (Penguin, 1972)
The New India by Ved Mehta (Penguin, 1978)
An Autobiography by M.K. Gandhi (Navajivan Publishing House, Ahmedabad)
Indian Tales and Legends by J.E.B. Gray (O.U.P., 1979)
Cradle Tales of Hinduism by Sister Nivedita (Advaita Ashrama, Calcutta, 1975)
The Far Pavilions by M.M. Kaye (Allen Lane, 1978)
Indian Vegetarian Cookery by Jack Santa Maria (Rider, 1973)

Amar Chitra Katha produce a wide range of comics in English which provide an entertaining and readable introduction to Indian history, the classics, mythology, folk tales and legends. (Available from India Book House, London.)

Index

The figures in **bold type** refer to pages on which illustrations appear